GAME-DAY GODDESS:
LEARNING FOOTBALL'S LINGO

Imagine receiving an invitation to your boss's party to watch a football game. Horror strikes because you don't know the first thing about the sport—or maybe you'd like to know more. Or, you love your job, and you want to impress your supervisor and colleagues. But what's a touchdown? Why are these men knocking each other down and charging about wildly?

Before you go nuts trying to learn the language of football on your own, read *Game-Day Goddess: Learning Football's Lingo* to understand the game. A handy reference covering the most important phrases used in today's game at the college and pro level, this concise dictionary features simple entries. With this resource, readers will never again be at a loss for the meaning of a football phrase or feel foolish because they don't know what's going on out on the field.

by Suzy Beamer Bohnert
Copyright © 2001, 2006, 2007
All Rights Reserved

Here's What Readers Are Saying About
Game-Day Goddess: Learning Football's Lingo

"A great read with terrific explanations for all the football terms."
-Philadelphia Eagles' Promotions Department

"We enjoyed the creative definitions. We use it as a reference source at women's events."
-Pittsburgh Steelers' Marketing/Community Relations Departments

"Having trouble keeping up with game-day banter? This is a lighthearted book and the resource you need. With humor and accuracy, Beamer Bohnert's glossary of handy phrases and terms is easy to use and places you among the informed."
-Virginia Tech Magazine

"I've been looking forever for a book like this!"
-Adamstown Area Library

"Many women will benefit from your book. Send my library a copy!"
-Everett Free Library

"The book is fun and makes for a very interesting discussion."
-Monroeville Public Library

"Now you can get in on the act, too, with this humorous guide to football. It gives an introduction to the sport for the uninitiated."
-Falls Church News-Press

"What a great idea. We really like it!"
-Virginia Tech Football Department

"Men, women, and children love this book because it's entertaining, funny, and informative. It's loaded with humor, easy to understand, and let's you learn about football painlessly."
-Culpeper Citizen

"The paperback tackles all aspects of the professional and college game humorously. A usable resource for anyone just learning the game."
-The Star News

"Brief and small enough to fit into a pocketbook to bring to a game. While the title points to a female target, the book is ideal for anyone who needs a little extra help with his or her football lingo."
-The Collegiate Times

Also by Suzy Beamer Bohnert

Binkie Learns to Fly

ISBN 978-1-4243-0299-4

Library of Congress Control Number: 2007901573
Library of Congress subject headings:
Football
Football—Dictionaries
Football—Humor
Sports—Dictionaries
Sports—Dictionaries—English
Games—Dictionaries

Cover designed by David Wu

Published by B&B Publishing

B&B Publishing
Visit our Web site and Author Online at http://mysite.verizon.net/vzeug7mn/
bandbpublishing@hotmail.com

Printed in the United States of America

DEDICATION

To Randall, Rand, and Carolyn, husband, son, and daughter, who were good sports during the research and writing of this book. Thanks for your encouragement and love.

To my parents, who stressed to their children the importance of recreation and suggested athletics as a creative outlet for our excess energy. You've provided a lifetime gift.

To my siblings, who were always good teammates and competitors.

PREFACE

After spending my early years after college as a sportswriter, I thought there was a need for such a book for women who enjoy football, but are reluctant to ask questions of others. You can't enjoy a game if you don't know enough about what's going on or are afraid to question people about what's happening.

To get women involved in the sport—so they're not left alone on the sidelines—I've written a humorous guide to the key phrases you'll hear on the radio or television football broadcasts. In simple words, you'll find the meanings to the game's language, enabling you to follow along.

Many thanks to reviewers Amy Silverman, Debbie Kahn Spiliotopoulos, and Bob Thorson for their excellent suggestions regarding revisions to the book. Thanks to David Wu for his artistic renderings, which grace this book's front and back covers.

A final thank you to the National Football League, which provided information and resources for this book.

OVERVIEW

Though football might look like a complicated game, if you understand a few simple concepts you'll get the hang of the sport without much hassle.

Let's begin with some basic material to give you a good start. Football teams have 11 players who play on offense and 11 players who play on defense. Each team puts out only its offense or defense on the field at one time. You will see the offense of one team opposing the defense of another when on the field.

The playing field is 100 yards in length with end zones at each end that are ten yards deep. Each end of the field belongs to one of the two teams. A team's offense wants to move in the direction of the other team's end of the field. A team's defense wants to prevent the other team from moving toward its end of the field.

The object of the game is to score more points than the opposing team because the team with the most points during a game wins.

So how does a team score? The team with the ball is on offense and has four downs, or attempts, to move the ball ten yards toward the opponent's end. A team can move the ball by running with it or by successfully passing it. An attempt or play continues until the defender tackles the ballcarrier or forces him off the field of play. If the offense does advance the ball ten yards within four tries, then they get another four attempts to move the ball downfield ten more yards. Each time the offense moves the ball downfield, it is getting closer to the opponent's end of the field, called the goal line. However, if a team can't move the ball ten yards in four tries, it must give the ball back to the other team, usually by kicking it to them.

The importance of the other team's goal line cannot be understated. This is where an offense scores its points! The goal line itself features a crossbar set back in an area called the end zone. The end zone is ten yards in length and has as its beginning the goal line where, if the ballcarrier crosses, it's a touchdown. The ballcarrier can run past the goal line or catch a pass beyond the goal line to score.

Scoring works in this fashion. Each time the ballcarrier passes the other team's goal line on a pass or a run, it's six points. If the defense intercepts a pass, recovers a fumble, or blocks a kick and, in each instance brings it over the opponent's goal line that, too, counts for six points.

Officials award points for different scoring options. For instance, if a team kicks the ball through the goalposts, this nets three points, and we call it a field goal. A safety, or two points, goes to a team on defense if it tackles the team on offense behind its own goal line. Six additional points accrue immediately after a team scores a touchdown. Following a touchdown a team has the option to go for one point or two. This is called a conversion attempt. A team gains two points if its offense successfully completes a two-yard run or pass play across the goal line.

One point goes to the offense if it kicks the ball through the goalposts after a touchdown.

Officials watch the play on the field to be sure rules are adhered to, and if they are not, the officials penalize the teams. Officials also keep track of the time, separating it into four quarters. After two quarters of play, a halftime occurs, where players on the field go into their locker room for coaching instruction, and marching bands or other such groups entertain the fans.

Of course, there are winners and losers in football and a way to keep track of those teams who make up the National Football League (NFL). The year 2002 brought some changes to the NFL in the way it divided its teams into different geographical divisions. With two different conferences already in place—the American Football Conference (AFC) and the National Football Conference (NFC)—this new plan aligned the teams into divisions of East, South, North, and West in both the NFC and the AFC.

Those squads in the NFC East Division are the following: Dallas; New York Giants; Philadelphia; and Washington. To make up the NFC South we have Atlanta, Carolina, New Orleans, and Tampa Bay. The NFC North consists of Chicago, Detroit, Green Bay, and Minnesota. Finally, we have Arizona, St. Louis, San Francisco, and Seattle in the NFC West.

On the AFC side, we have the East Division made up of the following teams: Buffalo; Miami; New England; and the New York Jets. The AFC South has Houston, Indianapolis, Jacksonville, and Tennessee as its components. The AFC North consists of Baltimore, Cincinnati, Cleveland, and Pittsburgh. Last, but not least, the AFC West has Denver, Kansas City, Oakland, and San Diego as its parts.

Plans are for a dozen teams to go to the playoffs. Teams are pitted against each other in divisional contests, with winners advancing, and a final game, known as the Super Bowl, played between the NFC champion and the AFC champion. The winner of the Super Bowl is considered the best team in all of professional football.

DEFINITIONS

Featuring all facets of the game, this portion of the book presents sports definitions, explaining complex notions in a simple way. Discussing phrases used to describe the offense and the defense, special teams, scoring, penalties, and signals, football followers will discover what they may have missed during game telecasts or afternoons in the stands.

Alphabetized for quick reference, many expressions common to college ball and the professional game appear.

Well, it's time to learn about definitions. Taking key words and phrases from the sports pages, television and radio broadcasts, and the fields where teams play everyday, we've put together a list of what you'll need to know to impress friends and family concerning your football knowledge.

What you thought the definition might mean appears in parentheses at the start of each definition. Italicized words appear as definitions on another page of the book.

A

AFC — (Not to be confused with ABCs.) Stands for American Football Conference, one part of the *National Football League*. The *National Football Conference* is the second of the league's two conferences.

against the grain — Signifies a *play* moving opposite of the movement of most other players on the *field*. This type of *play* typically develops near one of the *sidelines*.

alignment — (Nothing to do with your car's parts.) When you look at the defensive arrangement of a team's players on the *field*.

All-America — (What you hope your husband considers your efforts around the house.) Recognizing excellence of specific college football players, this award goes out every year to athletes selected for each of the positions on a team. Only the best players in the U.S. receive this tribute.

alley — (Forget the area where you park your car or dump your trash.) A defensive back hopes finding this crack in an offensive line will allow him to burst through and gain access to a favorite target—the guy who has the football.

angle block — Using your body to bulldoze a defensive player from the side, pushing him out of the play.

area blocking — Instead of picking out a particular player and stopping him, this strategy calls for *blocking* any competitor in a given area. See *zone blocking*.

artificial turf — (Similar to what you wish you had in your backyard, so you wouldn't have to mow the lawn.) Stadiums without grass have artificial turf, a covering designed to look like grass.

AstroTurf — A brand name for *artificial turf*.

audible — (Sorry, but not the loudness of your voice when the kids track mud on the new, white carpet, though your screaming may be clearly audible.) When the *quarterback* comes out of the *huddle* to start a *play*, or when the defense looks at the offensive setup, there might be a change of *play* or *formation* called out, which is different from what the *quarterback* or the defensive team leader calls in the *huddle*. When this last-second change happens, we call it an audible.

B

back — (Don't think chicken parts.) Three positions on the offensive team. These players have the responsibility of moving the ball forward by throwing, running, catching, or blocking, sometimes for a teammate who is already doing one of those activities during a play. *Quarterbacks*, *fullbacks*, and *halfbacks* typically fill these spots, but other common names for these positions include running back, *tailback*, *set back*, and flankerback.

backfield — Used to describe both the offense and the defense, this term defines those players, called the offensive backfield, who position themselves behind the offensive line and those athletes who place themselves behind the defensive line, known as the defensive backfield. An offensive backfield has the *quarterbacks*, *halfbacks*, and *fullbacks* throwing, blocking, running, and catching to move the ball down the field. In contrast, the defensive backfield, with its *cornerbacks* and *safeties*, aims to stop the *run* and any *pass* that comes toward them. Both backfields line up behind the linemen, who are in front.

backfield in motion — Tack on a five-yard *penalty* if someone on the offensive squad budges ahead of the *snap* or if two or more offensive players are stirring either horizontally or backward.

balanced formation — Features an offensive alignment with each side designated to take part in a specific *play*. For instance, a running *play* may feature *blockers* on the right side; if a throw is in mind for the *play*, the *receivers* line up on the opposite, or left side.

balanced line — (When the kids all show up for the church photo.) When the same number of people go to either side of the *center*, who lines up in the middle of the offensive *line*.

ball control — When a team can hold onto the ball for a long time, denying the opposition a chance to use its offense.

ball hawk — (Not a bird who mysteriously threw the ball through your favorite bay window, as the kids claim.) A skilled player on defense who gets the ball by *intercepting* it or *recovering* a *fumble*.

bat — (Something you hope your kids don't want as a pet.) To knock a ball down after an opponent's throw, or to knock a ball loose from a competitor's grasp.

beat the spread — (Hardly getting the butter to stay on the pancakes without dripping to the floor.) Gamblers liked to say if you wagered on a team that won or lost a game by a score greater or less than the *point spread* they estimated, you beat the spread, thus earning you money—for cosmetics.

belly series — (Grossly overweight men traveling together on the beach.) When the *quarterback* stuffs the ball into his *running back's* gut or *fakes* doing this on several plays on offense.

Big Ben — A *quarterback* may throw a pass to potential *receivers*, each of whom a defender covers, to win a game for the quarterback's team in the final minutes.

big play — Something to spur a team on, lifting its spirits, such as a *fumble*, or a pass play gaining tremendous *yardage* and moving the offense close to the *goal line*.

blast — (Saved for the child who used purple crayon on your Laura Ashley wallpaper.) For a player to gain crucial *yardage*, say in a situation with fourth down and a yard to go for a *first down*, a *running back* will blast defenders out of his way to allow a teammate to move forward.

blitz — A play by the defense, specifically a *linebacker* or a defensive back. On a passing situation, these players would try to get at the *quarterback* and hurry him to force a play. See *red-dog* and *shoot*.

block — A technique used to stop the *motion* of a player on the other team. This usually involves using the body or the shoulders because players on offense may not use their hands to block. This term also applies to preventing a kick or *pass* from going to its intended point.

blocking back — A player with the responsibility of blocking for a *running back* or *quarterback* during a play on offense.

blow a coverage — (And you thought it was when you forget to renew your insurance policy.) A phrase used both on offense and on defense to denote a mistake. For instance, on offense, if the *quarterback* does not identify *pass* coverages correctly, he could throw the ball to a *receiver* when he shouldn't because the pass catcher has a defender hanging all over him. On defense, a player may not cover his *receiver* well enough, or at all.

blow dead — When an official uses his whistle to stop play after the ball heads out of bounds, there's a *penalty*, or a team calls a *time-out*.

bomb squad — (If the kids are home with the baby sitter, place the number for this group by the phone.) A group of players who protect the principal players on a team during plays involving *punts*, *field goals*, or *kickoffs*. See *special team* or *suicide squad*.

bootleg — (Prohibition was a long time ago.) Involving the *quarterback* who takes the ball, pretends it will be a running play by faking a *handoff* to a *running back*, and then sneaks the ball on his hip, while running to one side of the field, to make a passing play.

box-and-chain crew — Workers who help the officials with the responsibility of keeping track of the *chain* used to measure for *first downs* and managing the down box.

break a tackle — (Your husband's excuse for not catching any fish, necessitating him going fishing again next weekend—leaving you alone with the kids.) A player who moves away from or overpowers a defender after he tries to make a *tackle* and then continues to run down the field.

break formation — On offense, at the opponent's 20-yard line and inward, a team will use this *formation* that has three players as *wide receivers*. By using various offensive ploys, such as *shifting* or movement, the wide receivers try to *fake* out the defense.

break off a run — Making a run on offense that goes through the defense, resulting in a big *yardage* gain.

breakaway — A run *downfield* that nets *yardage* and gets a player away from the defense.

broken play — (When the kids start a screaming match with their playmates, ending up in an argument.) When *signals* cross on offense and the *quarterback*, *running backs*, and *receivers* don't know what to do. Typically, this play results in a loss of *yardage* for the offense. See *busted play*.

bullet — (Nothing to do with ammunition.) A *pass* thrown by the *quarterback* with great force.

bump and run or bump and go — (Happens sometimes in the mornings when you and your husband are getting the kids ready for school, preparing lunches, and heading to work.) When a cornerback guards a *receiver*, he can bump him one time during a play to get him off balance, so the receiver can't catch the ball. After bumping the *receiver*, the *cornerback* will still try to run *downfield* to cover the *receiver* during a pass play.

burner — (You're thinking something to do with the stove.) A player on offense with great speed.

busted play — (When your child's friend can't come over to play after all.) The same thing as a broken play. When things get confused on offense for some key players, and the play usually results in lost *yardage*. See *broken play*.

butt-blocking — The officials assess a 15-yard *penalty* for any play where a player pushes a helmet or *face mask* into an opposing athlete.

buttonhook — When a *receiver* goes *downfield* in a straight line and then quickly turns back around to face his *quarterback* to catch a *pass*.

C

center — His position is in the middle of the offensive line. He starts the offensive play by *hiking* the ball through his legs backward to waiting teammates.

center line — A white line dividing the *field* into halves that goes across the middle of the field.

center snap — (What two adults might do when encountering a misbehaving child at the dinner table lodged in between them.) The play on offense starts when the *center* takes the ball and throws it, or hands it, through his legs to teammates behind him.

chain — (Not something you use on Rover.) Also known as a *yardage chain*. This chain, moved by game personnel, is ten yards long, the distance an offense must move in four plays to keep the ball. Personnel keep the chain on the sidelines to see if, indeed, a team has gone that distance. See *yardage chain* or *sticks*.

chalk talk or chalk session — (For the child who used chalk on your favorite Monet.) A coach discusses plays and approaches, sometimes using chalk and a blackboard to illustrate and to help his team understand. See *skull session* or *skull practice*.

chop block — (What you do to pork, so it doesn't hit the floor as you trim it for your next meal.) Hitting an opponent at or below the knees. An illegal play resulting in a *penalty* of 15 yards.

chuck — (Not a form of beef.) A player on defense will jostle a *receiver* by hitting him with outstretched forearms in front of his body—this is legal, as long as the hit comes within three yards of the *line of scrimmage* and takes place only once.

circle pattern or circle route — (Don't think sewing.) Sending a *receiver* on offense to catch a *pass* after he goes *upfield* and circles in toward the *field's* middle.

clearing route — (Happens when Mom makes her way from the kitchen to the dining room, bringing a hot dish to the table.) A *running back*, as a decoy, runs a clearing route, hoping to lure defenders to cover him, leaving other *receivers* open *downfield*.

clip — (Shorten the bangs, please.) A 15-yard *penalty* arises for knocking down a player by hitting his legs from behind, provided this player is not the ballcarrier, and this doesn't happen within a specified *zone* that allows clipping.

clock play — To manage time near the end of a *quarter* the offense will usually call a *pass play*, requiring a *receiver* to be near the *sidelines*. If the player on offense catches the *pass*, the *receiver* will step *out of bounds, stopping the clock.* Even if the *pass* is *incomplete*, the clock still stops.

clothesline — (Associated with clean laundry.) An illegal play involving a defender putting out his arm to stop the ballcarrier and catching him under the chin.

coffin corner — Traditionally, a punter will aim for this area, which is a corner near the *sideline* and the other team's *goal line*. Once kicked, if the ball lands in the *field* in this coffin-corner spot and then goes *out of bounds*, it will be near the opposition's own *goal line*, giving that squad's offense poor field position.

College Football Hall of Fame — Collegiate football honors the best football players to have played the game at this site in Kings Island, Ohio. Viewers can see the displays throughout the year.

color — (When doing laundry, don't to forget to separate the whites from the darks, or your results will be this.) Provided by a sports broadcaster, who adds information to the telecast to spice it up, including *statistics*, a breakdown of what's happening on the *field*, and an evaluation of play. Also called a *color commentator*.

color commentator — A counterpart to the play-by-play broadcaster. This person provides statistics, an analysis of what's happening on the field, and an evaluation of *play*. Also called *color*.

combination coverage — (When you run an errand while your husband baby-sits. Eventually you relieve him when you get back, allowing him to head out on tasks.) If you have two *receivers* on offense, both lining up on different sides of the *field*, the defense in this coverage will *guard* one receiver *man-for-man* and will double-team the other.

compensation — (What you feel you need more of from your boss.) Many player contracts have "an option," allowing a team to use the same terms of an expired player contract for an extra year. If the player decides to move on to a new team, the new team he goes to will pay cash to the old team he played for, give up future *draft picks*, or both.

complete or completion or connect — (When you and your blind date have a good time.) On offense, a *pass* caught by a *receiver*.

conversion — After making a touchdown, to earn one point, a team can kick the ball through the *goalposts*. Or to gain two *points*, they can run or complete a pass into the *end zone* from two yards out. We call these *extra points* conversions.

corner blitz — A play by one or both defensive *cornerbacks*, in a passing situation, to get at the *quarterback* and hurry him to force a play.

corner route — When a *receiver* on offense runs *downfield* and then heads diagonally to the *goal-line flag*, in the corner of the *field*, to catch a *pass*.

cornerback — (Where dust bunnies form in your living room—the corner, in back.) Lining up on the other side of the *linebacker*, this player on defense tries to *tackle* the ballcarrier on running plays and *guard* the *receivers* on *passing plays*.

cough up — A mistake where the offense drops the ball, turning it over to the other team. Often the offense turns the ball over because of a good defensive effort to get the ball away.

count — (Useful to do before losing your temper.) Determined in the *huddle* by the *quarterback*, this secret word or sound lets his players know when the *center* will *snap* the ball, beginning the play.

counter — A *play* to *fake* out the defense, where the offense has the ballcarrier go in the opposite direction of where its other players head. For instance, if the players head left, the ballcarrier will run to the right.

crab block — (Prohibiting a cranky child from leaving the house.) Some call this a body block, and it is when a *tackler* uses his side rather than his shoulders to plow into an opposing runner.

crackback — (Happens when you try to exercise.) A play made on a *linebacker* or defensive back resulting in a block considered illegal.

cross — (Mood after your mate forgot your birthday.) A pass *receiver* on each side of the *field* runs straight ahead and then veers toward the center of the field, crossing paths with the offensive *receiver* from the other side.

cross block — On offense, a lineman will cross paths with another lineman as they go about blocking. See *scissors*.

cross buck — (What your daughter will feel if her allowance doesn't go up by a dollar a week.) To fool the opponents, two *running backs* will each head toward the front line at a *slant*, eventually crossing in front of one another. By the *quarterback* pretending to give the ball to one *running back*, while handing it off to the other, he often misleads the defense.

cross tackle — When a player *tackles* an opponent by grabbing his waist with the arms and throwing his body against an opponent's legs to drag him down.

crossing pattern — Also known as a cross, a *pass receiver* on each side of the *field* runs straight ahead and then veers toward the center of the field, crossing paths with the offensive *receiver* from the other side.

crossover or crossover step — (Used to avoid toys on the floor in the kitchen.) A move requiring some coordination, this involves lifting the leg and swinging it over the other, usually when an athlete goes sideways or has to go in an opposite direction.

curbstone coach — Also known as Monday morning *quarterback*, armchair *quarterback*, or grandstand *quarterback*. Done by many fans who provide opinions to the players from the comfort of their living room, after the game, or from the stands, as to what the *quarterback* should have done on a specific play or in a certain situation.

curl or curl-in — (Hair terminology.) Used to gain sure *yardage* and to lessen the risk of *interception*, this *pass play* on offense has the *receiver* head *downfield*, then suddenly turn back to face the *quarterback*, who throws the ball to the *receiver* immediately.

cut — (Suffered by child after falling off the Jungle gym.) This term has several uses. For instance, a team may cut a player, which means that athlete lost his job and no longer plays for that squad. Another usage indicates when a player on offense tries to wiggle free from an opponent. Finally, we hear the term used to indicate when someone on offense tries to get away to catch a *pass*.

cut block — Early in the development of an offensive play, a defender will trip a *receiver*, who is trying to get away to make a catch.

cutoff block — (Chopping apart the baby's toy after you twisted your ankle as a result of stumbling over it.) Using the body as a human roadblock, the *center*, who plays on offense, will throw himself in front of a defensive lineman, stopping the opponent dead in his tracks and allowing a *running back* to move forward on a run.

D

D back — (Subject to aches and pains.) This term refers to a defensive back.

dead ball — (The way you feel each night after taking care of work, kids, and husband.) When the officials stop play, halting movement of the ball by a *run*, *pass*, kick, or *return*. A ball is also dead when there's no time left on the game clock, when a *penalty* occurs, or when a *quarter* ends.

dead-man play — An illegal play—sometimes referred to as a *hideout* or *sleeper play*—where a team member on offense pretends to head to the *sidelines* where his teammates are located, but ends up staying along that *sideline* to act as a *pass receiver*. See *hideout* and *sleeper play*.

decline a penalty — (What your kids want to do when you're disciplining them.) When a *penalty* occurs against a team, the captain of the opposing team can decide whether or not to accept the *penalty*. Because it is sometimes advantageous for the opposing team to let the existing play stand as is, the choice will be to decline the *penalty*.

deep drop — (What you do with stinky garbage.) To not be hit and *tackled* by opposing players, a *quarterback* readies himself for a *pass play* by running back a few steps from the *line of scrimmage*, enabling him to have a clear view *downfield* to see his pass catchers.

defensive end — These athletes make charging the *quarterback* and watching for *running plays* going toward the *sidelines* their specialty. Most teams have two of these players, who line up on the outermost side of the *defensive tackles* at the *line of scrimmage*.

defensive tackle — Like the defensive ends, these guys go after the *quarterback*, but they also *guard* against *running plays* that are heading toward the middle of the *field*. Typically, there are two on a squad, and they line up between the defensive ends at the *line of scrimmage*.

defensive team — Any time you hear the words defense, defensive unit, or "D," they are talking about the people who make up the defensive squad out on the playing *field*.

delay of game — (Happens when you can't find the pieces to the family's favorite, Monopoly) Officials slap a team with a five-yard *penalty* if it doesn't start a play on offense within a certain time.

depth chart — (A list of who's available to accompany you to the wedding for which you have an invitation.) This is a way for the management of the team to note who's the top performer in each player-position slot, who's the next most talented in that position, and so on.

diamond defense — (For the engagement ring that just wasn't the carat size you wanted, here's your fiancé's out.) On defense, this refers to the *free safety*, the nose guard, and the two interior *linebackers*.

dime defense — (When your husband didn't spend much money on your birthday gift, this is his excuse.) When you see six defensive backs out on the *field* for a defense.

disabled list — When a player's name appears on this list it means he is still a part of the squad, but he is hurt and not fit to play. Facing no *penalty*, a team can reinstate another player in the injured player's place.

dive — (Your male friend's residence.) A running play where the player who has the ball tries to leap over defenders, going forward to gain a few yards.

diveback — (Someone who moved in with a girlfriend, left her, and went back to his original residence.) When using the *I formation*, this term notes the *fullback*.

double coverage — (Lining up two dates for one night. If one flops, there's always the other.) Also known as double-team, this is when two teammates on the defense get together to cover one man on the offense.

double-double zone defense — In a passing situation, you have *zone* coverage when defensive players protect certain parts of the *field* and defend against opponents who come in that section of the *field*. Doubling up the number of players on defense who cover each side of the *field* is double-double *zone* defense.

double motion — (The move you make when you and your friend head to the powder room at the same time.) When a player in the *backfield* on offense moves in a different direction from the path in which he was first moving—legal, as long as it is behind the *line of scrimmage*.

double reverse — (Heading, with a friend, in opposite directions to avert the nerd heading toward you to ask you out.) During the first segment of this *play*, the *quarterback* hands the ball to another player on offense, who heads in the opposite direction of the *quarterback*. This player then gives the ball to a second teammate, who runs in the same direction as the *quarterback* who started the *play*, creating a second, or double reverse, confusing the defense.

double-slot formation — This formation on offense has a player placed between the *tight end* and the *tackle* and a second player between the *split end* and the other *tackle*.

double wing — (Deformed piece of chicken.) You will see this on offense and know this *formation* is in use when you notice two *halfbacks*—each of whom is playing as a *receiver*—and a *split end*.

down — (Happens when you have a bad-hair day.) When the offense has the ball, it gets four tries to go forward ten yards. If it's successful, it gets another four attempts, or downs. Another usage indicates the tackling of the ballcarrier, signaling a play's end.

down-and-in — (Occurs when you show up at work, but really wanted a mental-health day.) On offense, a *receiver* will jet *downfield* and swerve inward toward the center of the field, expectantly eluding the defender on this *pass route*.

down-and-out — On offense, a *receiver* will jet *downfield* and swerve outward toward the closest *sideline*, expectantly eluding the defender on this *pass route*.

down lineman — (A lineman from the power company who fell down.) The *center*, *tackles*, and *guards* on offense and defense.

downfield — This is the direction the team on offense wants to go. They want to move forward, or downfield.

downfield blocking — When a play develops, sometimes it moves *downfield* where there are fewer players, though it is necessary to have downfield blocking from players on offense, so the runner can waltz into the *end zone* untouched.

draft — (What your mate has as a beverage during all sporting events.) A process where the pro teams select the college football players at an event. A certain selection process determines the pick of these athletes. First, *National Football League* (*NFL*) officials look at each team's win-loss record for the last season.

Then they assign each team a number, which indicates the order in which they pick in the draft. The team with the poorest win-loss record in the *NFL* gets to choose the first player. The team that won the previous season's Super Bowl picks last. The process provides the opportunity for the poorest teams to snatch up some of the finest prospects before the better teams have their chance to choose.

When an organization picks a player, this allows the team to talk to him exclusively. If the athlete and the team can't agree on contract specifics, that opens the door for other franchises to talk to that athlete and put him on their roster. But this only happens if the team that wants him gives the team that drafted him some future draft picks or players as reimbursement. Of course, a team can waive its right to pick a player, too, passing its chance to draft a player to another team, who gives it players or future draft picks.

draw — When a player on defense goes over the *line of scrimmage* prematurely because a player on offense lured him over by making a gesture or maneuver that made the defensive player think the play had started.

draw play — (Using several different crayons on that Laura Ashley wallpaper.) When the *quarterback* fades back several steps from the *front line*, giving everyone the impression he's going to throw the ball, and then he belatedly gives the ball to a *running back* instead for a *running play*.

drive — (All your kids want you to do these days—school, soccer, friend's house.) The object of the game is for the offense to keep moving forward toward the opponent's end of the field until the offense scores. This term just means the offense is moving forward consistently.

drive-block — A necessary *block* to make way for a ballcarrier by pushing a defender backward.

drop back — (A dress with a low backline.) On offense, a *quarterback* will shuffle backward several steps to get ready to *pass* the ball *downfield*.

duck or duck ball or dying quail — (A main course.) When a toss doesn't have a tight spiral, making it susceptible to *interception* because it lacks speed and power, it merely drifts.

E

eat the ball — A situation where some defenders are about to *tackle* the *quarterback* behind the *line of scrimmage*. The *quarterback* decides not to throw a *pass*, fearing an *interception*, and not to *run* forward with the ball, fearing a *fumble*. Instead, he decides to grip the ball firmly, putting his head down, allowing the defenders to tackle him on the spot for a loss.

eight-man front — When a team puts out four defensive linemen and four *linebackers* to defend against the offense.

eleven — (Number of times you go out to dinner in a decade.) The number of players on offense and the number on defense.

eligible receiver — (Someone worthy of your affectionate glances.) On offense, the rules allow *running backs* and the *ends*—sometimes known as a *tight end* and another called a *split end*—to grab *forward passes* thrown by the *quarterback*. Any time, however, the defense tips or touches the ball during a play, any athlete on offense can catch it.

encroaching — (Hitting on someone's boyfriend.) Results in a five-yard *penalty* when a player crosses the *line of scrimmage* with any body part while getting ready for the *hike* of the football from the *center* to the *quarterback*. A player can also receive the same *penalty* if he touches a player on the other team while getting ready for the *hike*, but before the *snap* of the ball from *center*.

end — Players on offense or defense with very distinct roles. Operating on offense, these players usually play one of two spots— *split end* or *tight end*. Their role on offense is to *block* oncoming defenders during *running plays*, and on other plays, to catch *passes*. In either case, they line up as the last player on the line, hence the term end. When playing defense, the ends try to crush the *quarterback* by charging in on him or pouncing on the runner when he heads toward the *sidelines*, rather than down the middle of the *field*.

end around — An *end* not only *blocks* and catches *passes*, but he also completes *running plays*. Especially sneaky is the end around, requiring the *end* to retreat into the *backfield* where the *quarterback* is, take the ball from him, and *run* toward the side of the *field* where the other *end* lined up, sprinting past him and then *downfield*.

end run — Like the *end around*, this play has the runner skirt defenders by darting out toward the *sidelines* and around the *end* on a *running play*.

end zone — Between the *goal line* and end line on both ends of the *field* lies an area where they have written a team's name. This area is ten yards deep.

even defense — Means a team has an even—rather than an odd number—of *down linemen* on the *field*.

expansion team — (A group of friends who have gained weight.) A good example of an expansion team is the Carolina Panthers. They filled a void, adding to the *National Football League* another club in a different city, growing the league. To get players on the roster to go play for this organization based in Charlotte, N.C., the *NFL* conducted a *draft*, giving the Panthers an opportunity to select players in a pool of unprotected athletes available from all league teams.

extra point — (Awarded when your "significant other" compliments your new hairstyle.) Only possible after a team scores a *touchdown*. One extra point goes to a team if it kicks the ball through the *goalposts*, and it gets two points if it makes good on a pass attempt or a run into the *end zone* from two yards out. See *conversion*.

F

face-guarding — (Applying enough make-up so no one sees your new pimple.) A form of *pass interference*. On defense, those guarding the offensive *receivers* need to watch that they don't blind the *receiver* by flapping their arms to distract a *receiver's* view. The defender must play the ball and not the *receiver*. If the defender fails to do so, the offense gets the ball and a *first down* at the point where the *penalty* happened.

face protector — Also known as a *face mask*, this plastic grid shields players from injuries to the face.

face mask — (Cleansing cream worn at night.) On each helmet, a plastic grid shields players from injuries to the face. If a player pulls on this to drag a runner to the ground, it results in a 15-yard *penalty* and a *loss of down*, if done intentionally. For an unintentional occurrence, there is a replay of *down* and a five-yard loss of yardage.

face-masking — A team receives a *penalty* when a player on offense or defense grabs a player's *face mask* to move him out of the way or *tackle* him. For this violation, tack on a 15-yard *penalty*. If grasping the *face mask* of the runner or the *quarterback*, chalk up a five-yard assessment.

fair catch — (An average date with a man.) By signaling for a fair catch, this allows a player to catch a ball booted by the opposing squad without *interference*. Usually, an athlete decides to fair catch because it gives him a better chance of catching the ball after an onslaught of defenders comes sprinting downfield to *tackle* him and only him. Hoisting an arm in the air during the ball's travel downfield signals a fair catch and means the opposition cannot touch him, and he can't *run* the ball afterward. However, if the player tries to catch the ball and *fumbles*, or has the ball touch him and roll away, then anyone can recover the ball. Wherever the competitor catches the ball after a fair catch, that's where the next *play* starts.

fake — (Not real, such as false eyelashes.) Pretending to steer one way, but heading the opposite way. Used frequently on offense by *running backs* and *quarterbacks*, *pass receivers* and punters.

false start — (When you go to kiss your date and he backs away.) Chalk up a five-yard *penalty* against the offense when one of its participants on the *line of* *scrimmage* budges after positioning himself for play, thus making others believe the *play* started.

false trap — Making the offensive linemen *block* as if the play executed were a *sweep play* or a trap *play*, which leaves a gaping hole for the runner to plunge through because the defender vacates his position to follow the blockers. See *sucker trap*.

field — Each football field is the same length—120 yards—and rectangular. The playing area is 100 yards long, but two *end zones*, one at each end of the field, take up the other 20 yards. You can easily identify the *end-zone* areas because markings appear with the name of one of the teams that is playing and the *goalposts* are there. The field is 53.5 yards in width, and lines mark the *sidelines* of the field, the *end zone*, and five-yard intervals from one end of the field to the other.

field goal — When a team isn't close enough to score a *touchdown*, it may try a field goal, which adds three points to a squad's score. A field goal happens when a player kicks the ball above the crossbar and between the *goalposts* located in the opposing team's *end zone*.

field judge — Most of this official's duties involve looking at *passing plays* and *punt* situations. He will examine if *pass interference* occurred on a *play*, or whether a *punt* went *out of bounds* at one spot or another, or whether someone signaled for a *fair catch*. Keeping tabs on the offense getting off the *play* in time, and watching the time allotted for *time-outs* and halftime are also duties of the field judge.

find — (A real catch.) Looking *downfield*, locating a *receiver*, and then having that *receiver* catch a *pass*.

first-and-ten — (The first of ten blind dates.) *First down* with ten yards to go.

first down — A team's first chance on offense at moving forward ten yards in four attempts to keep the ball. If the team accomplishes this, they get to retain the ball for another four downs.

first-stringer — The team's best players, who begin the game in the lineup.

flag — (Tied to your car when it breaks down during rush hour.) By throwing a handkerchief-sized flag out of their pockets, the officials signal when a player's broken one or more rules of the game.

flag on the play — When a tossed handkerchief-sized flag appears on the *field* because someone broke the game rules.

flagrant foul — (When the baby's diaper needs changing.) Infractions, serious in nature, resulting in 15-yard *penalties*. These include *clipping*, intentional *face mask*, or kicking.

flak jacket — (For those with no sense of fashion.) Designed for players who want to spare their upper body, chest, and rib area from harm. This is a vest worn with padding.

flanker — (Has to do with meat and the butcher shop.) On offense, an athlete who is some distance from the *running backs* and *quarterback* and who plans to catch a *pass* rather than *run* the ball. See *split end*, *spread end*, or *wide receiver*.

flare — (Used for auto emergencies.) Geared to gain *yardage* by *passing* the ball toward the *sideline* to a *running back* who is near the *line of scrimmage*.

flat — An imaginary spot on offense, primarily a pass-reception area, to the right or left of a *formation*.

flea-flicker — (Method of ridding the dog of insects.) During the first segment of this play, the *quarterback* hands the ball to a *running back*, who *fakes* a running play and then gives the ball back to the *quarterback*. The *quarterback* then gets the ball and passes it *downfield* to a waiting *receiver*.

flex defense — A situation where defenders backpedal from the *line of scrimmage* just before the *play's* start because they anticipate a *running play* by the offense.

flip-flop — (Worn on the feet to the pool.) A team wants the best *defensive tackles* matched up against the side where the offense has the most players—accomplished, sometimes, by a squad moving the *safeties* to the *linebacker's* spot or vice versa before the *play* starts.

flood — (Happens frequently in your basement.) A strategy to increase the chances of having the offense catch the ball by sending some players to the same section of the *field*, outnumbering the defenders there and increasing the odds of a *completion*.

football knee — Football's a punishing sport, often damaging an athlete's cartilage or ligaments because of the excessive pounding players take when *tackled*.

force man — (Pushing your mate to do chores around the house.) On a *run* by the offense toward the *sideline* either the *linebacker*, *strong safety*, or *cornerback* earns a paycheck by forcing this *play* toward the middle of the *field*.

formation — (Happens to leftovers in Tupperware.) Before starting a *play* on offense or defense, the competitors will position themselves on the *field* in what we call a formation. Not what they taught you in geology about rocks.

forward lateral — A legal *lateral* is an underhand or overhand *pass* of the ball from one player to the next that must go sideways or backwards before the *line of scrimmage*. A lateral going forward past the *line of scrimmage* incurs a *penalty* of five yards and a *loss of down*.

forward pass — (When a man aggressively tries to catch your attention.) An overhand pass of the ball from a player to another eligible player farther *downfield*. Any legitimate forward *pass* requires its launch from behind the *line of scrimmage* only once on each *play*.

foul — (Something that smells bad.) Violation of the game rules, resulting in *yardage* taken away from a team or a combination of lost *yardage* and a *loss of down* assessed against a team.

four-three defense — When a team has two *ends* and two *tackles* on the *front line*—note how they lean down on their hands on the *front line*—plus three *linebackers*.

fourth down — A final chance for the offense to move the ball forward for a total of ten yards if the first three tries come up short.

free agent — Once a contract expires, or if a player doesn't have one, an athlete is free to play for any team.

free ball — (Charity athletic event.) When the ball ambles about and no one has *possession* of it, but anyone's entitled to it if they can grab it.

free kick — Typically takes place after a score by *field goal*, *safety*, or two-point conversion, at the game's beginning, and following halftime.

free safety — A roving player on defense whose job it is to assist his squad on *run* or *pass plays* to any area of the *field*. At the start of a *play*, he usually positions himself across from the side with fewer players on the offensive *line*. See *weak safety*.

freeze — (To put in the top part of the refrigerator.) When a team is beating another by a slim margin it will try to hold on to the ball as long as it can, so the other squad can't try and score, thus freezing the other team out.

front — (Where your blouse buttons.) Consists of the defensive *line*.

front four — Four players on defense who comprise the defensive *line*.

front line — Competitors on offense or defense who play on the *line of scrimmage*.

front wall — (What you'd like to build so the neighbor's kids don't come over anymore.) Another name for the defensive linemen.

full house — (Having company.) On offense, placing the *halfbacks* and *fullbacks*—also called *tailback*, *setback*, and flankerback—in the *backfield*, so there are four there.

fullback — Primarily responsible for running the ball and blocking on offense, this player lines up behind the *quarterback*.

fumble — (What happens when you don't have your glasses on and you're trying to find them on the nightstand.) Different from a muff, this signals when a player doesn't hold on to the ball during a running play or *handoff* and turns the ball over to the other team. Often a costly mistake, the other squad gets to *run* with the ball as soon as they pick up the fumble and then keep the ball on offense.

G

gadget or gadget play — Designed to confuse the defense, these are special plays with unusual features.

gain — Positive *yardage* awarded after a *play* moves forward on offense.

game ball — An award to recognize the achievements of a coach or player during a win by that individual's team.

game films — (Videos you put in the VCR to give you some peace and quiet while the kids watch.) The coaching staff and squad review films to reveal weaknesses and strengths of individual players and teams. The films are sometimes helpful in designing strategies to defeat an opponent.

game plan — (Your strategy to leave the kids with the baby sitter before the littlest knows you're gone.) How a team plans to play its opponent both on offense and on defense by taking into account the other squad's personnel. A team's lineup will employ these ideas throughout a game, fine-tuning them as time goes on.

gamer — While proving adequate in practice, but not outstanding, this athlete executes superbly in game situations.

gang-tackle — (When the neighborhood children come to bully your kid.) When the defense gathers its players to *tackle* the opponent with the ball.

gap blocking — (Visually trying to eliminate the space between your date's teeth, which were knocked out with a hockey puck.) On the defensive *line*, the linemen want to leave no space to allow players on the offensive *line* to break through.

giveaway football — (Loaning the television to a neighbor on weekends from August through January.) A sloppy game distinguished by errors, including missed *tackles*, blown *pass* coverages, *interceptions*, *fumbles*, and chaos.

goal line — (What you want your husband to finish from the to-do list on lined paper on your refrigerator.) After a carried ball passes the opponent's goal line or someone catches a thrown ball over this line, it's considered a *touchdown*.

goal-line stand — Stopping an offense from scoring even when it is so close to the *goal line* that the defense must mount a considerable effort to keep the offense from doing so.

goalpost — Situated on the end line at each end of the *field*. Shaped so these two posts are vertical, connected by a crossbar, which kickers use as a visual when trying to boot the ball through the goalposts and over the crossbar when attempting a *field goal* or *extra-point*.

goal-to-go — A normal playing condition has a team moving forward ten yards to achieve a *first down*. However, if a team is so close to the opponent's *goal line* that it has less than ten yards before it ends up in the *end zone*, there's no chance to achieve another *first down*, and we call this goal-to-go.

go for it — (Reaching over and planting a kiss on the love of your life, even if it is only your first date.) If a team feels confident as it faces a *fourth-down* situation, or desperate to catch up with little time remaining, it will strive to gain the required *yardage* to keep the ball for another set of *downs*. The choice is either that or *punt* the ball to the other team.

go long — Going for broke with a *pass* thrown far *downfield*.

grasp-and-control rule — (When your children need just a little discipline.) *NFL quarterbacks* take a beating. To minimize the risk of these athletes acquiring more broken limbs than necessary, the rules stipulate a game *referee* can judge when a *quarterback* appears in the "grasp" of a defender. After the referee decides this, the ball's movement stops at that point, and the opponent gets a *sack* rather than a cheap shot at the *quarterback*.

grind out — (Method to get grass stains out of white shorts.) Putting the *running back* to work, an offense will have him *run* the ball numerous times to produce small gains and use up a lot of remaining game time. In an attempt to make sure there are no *turnovers*, sometimes a team will emphasize a strategy of no risky *pass* plays, thus grinding it out.

ground game — (Why your lawn is brown instead of green; the kids are always playing on it.) Instead of passing plays, this emphasizes rushing, keeping the ball on the ground, not in the air.

guard — (Sits in a chair at the pool watching your kids. Looks amazingly young.) Key blockers on the offensive line who try to generate gaping holes for the *running* *back*, who springs through them. When lining up, these blockers assume their offensive-line position, placing themselves on either side of the *center*. Used also as a verb, a player guards another when he tries to prevent the other player from catching a *pass* or succeeding at scoring.

gut — (Expanding stomach because of too much beer.) The middle of the offensive or defensive *line*.

H

halfback — A counterpart to the *fullback*. He lines up in the *backfield*, behind the *quarterback*, where other *running backs*, such as the *tailback* or *fullback*, play. The halfback carries the ball on *running plays* and catches passes. He's typically not as large as the *fullback* because the "halfback's" role requires more finesse rather than the sheer brute strength of the *fullback*.

Hail Mary — (Said with rosary in hand.) With the grace of God, this desperation *pass* flows through the air to someone who catches it, a good thing, provided the passer and *receiver* are on the same team. A ball thrown into a crowd of defenders to potential *receivers*. See *prayer*.

Hall of Fame — (Where you think you belong because of all you do.) A museum honoring the finest of both collegiate and professional football players and coaches. In some cases, the Hall of Fame recognizes the *National Football League's* coaches, teams, owners, and supporters.

handoff — (What you tell your kids when they get close to the Waterford crystal bowl.) Taking the ball and shoving it in the stomach area of the player. An activity occurring on offense.

hang time — (The amount of time it takes for the flowers that special someone gave you to go limp.) After a team fails to advance the ball ten yards, it *punts*, or kicks the ball, to the opposing team. By clocking the seconds the ball remains in the air after the kick, you can determine the hang time. Long hang time is desirable to enable the kicking team to go *downfield* and tackle the receiving player.

head butt — (When you feel your head and rear are about the same size.) A way to get an opponent's dentist upset, but a successful play where a player gets knocked on the chin with a swift helmet hit.

headhunter — (Used when searching for a new job.) Not a gentle individual—someone who's out for blood. A player who tends to be violent.

head linesman — (Someone the kids use to get the blue stripes straight in their newest punk-rocker haircut.) An official with a number of responsibilities, including watching for *penalties* at the *line of scrimmage*; managing the *chain* crew, who measure for *first-down yardage* and keep track of downs; spotting the ball from

isolated camera — (A hidden camera you need in your house to figure out who's eating all the cookies before mealtime.) Highlighting behavior on the *field* by means of videotape, allowing the viewing audience at home or the fans at the stadium to see, so they may judge the results of a specific *play* or event.

isolation block — (Applying restrictions to the child snacking before mealtime after you determined who it was via your camera.) After a *back* on offense notices a defender still moving about freely, that *back* will key in on that defender and *block* him squarely, even though the *back* may be slow in making the *block*.

J

jumper — (A baby who won't lie down.) To *bat* down the ball so it doesn't go through the *goalposts*. This defensive player leaps high in the air during a kicker's attempt at an *extra-point* effort following a score.

K

keeper — (A good man.) After pretending the *play* will be one in which the *running back* will carry the ball, the *quarterback* keeps the ball himself and runs with it.

key block — (Someone who makes conversation with a man you'd prefer to avoid, thus sparing you having to greet him.) A necessary block to make a *play* successful.

kicking game — (Used to get rid of an ex-lover.) Evaluating those who kick for the team, in any fashion, and rating their effectiveness.

kicking team — (A group of women who have gotten rid of an ex-lover.) Individuals who, on the *field*, are responsible for *punts, kickoffs, extra points,* and *field goals.*

kickoff — (Physically dismissing an unwanted advance.) One team will kick the ball to the other team to start the game, at the beginning of the second half, and whenever a team scores a *touchdown* or makes a *field goal*. Generally, the ball is held up on a tee placed at the *offensive team's* 30-yard line and kicked as far to the defensive end of the *field* as possible, so that the other team has poor *field* position.

kickoff return — (Physically dismissing an unwanted advance and having him try again.) Catching a football after the *kickoff* and running it toward the *end zone* of the other team.

L

lanes (running) — (Jogging path.) Ten fictitious *holes* spreading widthwise across the *field* used for running plays on offense.

late hit — (Someone you realized a moment too late is coming your way to ask you for a date.) A 15-yard *penalty* can be called against a team if a player goes to *tackle* a downed opponent after the end of a *play*. If the *play* is over and the player attacked is *out of bounds*, this is also considered a *penalty*.

lateral — (Something you hope your career moves are not.) On a given *play*, any number of these sideways passes can take place to any player on a team.

lead block — (Snubbing someone who feels he should be the most important person in your life.) A player helps his teammate by throwing a *key block* to pave the way for the ballcarrier to advance the ball.

leg whip — (When the chicken you made for dinner falls in the whip cream.) When a player extends his leg in a desperation move to trip his opposition, he gets a 10-yard *penalty*.

line — (A mistruth told by a man to get you to believe he's got more on the ball than he does.) There's one of these lines on offense and defense. On offense, the line has these players on it: a *center*, two *ends*, two *tackles*, and two *guards*. On defense, look for two *defensive tackles* and two *defensive ends*, plus maybe a middle *guard*.

line buck — (Disbelieving the dialogue you just had with a man who strikes you as insincere.) To gain short *yardage*, a player on offense leaps over his linemen or gets the tackles in front of him to clear opponents from his path.

line judge — (Outside confidantes who gauge the truthfulness of the dialogue you just had with a man.) An official looking for violations of *passing plays*—particularly to make sure *lateral passes* occur, without the *quarterback* stepping beyond the *line of scrimmage*. He'll also monitor for *offside* and encroachment problems. One last duty includes keeping track of time.

line of scrimmage — (The struggle to figure out if what a man tells you is true.) The spot from where each *play* begins, determined by where action halted on the previous *play*.

line surge — (Increased belief that what a man tells you is not true.) Occurs when the *center* takes the ball and *hikes* it to the *quarterback*, causing forward momentum by the offensive line, who try to *run* together as a group, blowing out an open path for the ballcarrier galloping behind them.

linebacker — (Another man who backs his male friend's gross conversational inaccuracies during a conversation with you.) These players are busy with the defensive assignment of stopping the runner on a rushing *play* and watching to make sure the *running backs* don't catch a *pass* in a passing situation.

linesman — (A man who tells gross conversational inaccuracies.) This official notes where the ball heads *out of bounds* and when there is an *offside* or encroachment occurrence.

live ball — (A spirited dance.) Once play starts from the *line of scrimmage*, you have a live ball.

look-in — (Checking in on your newborn while he sleeps.) A player runs across the *field* diagonally, and the *quarterback* dumps off a *pass* to him.

look off — (Turning away from your newborn as he sleeps after you realize his diaper's full.) When a *quarterback* glances over to one area of the *field* as he prepares to *pass* to a *receiver* on the opposite side.

loop — (If you sew, you will know this term.) When a lineman on defense charges into the offensive *line* to a position other than where he typically *plays*, resulting in a confused offensive *line*.

loose — (What you wish your pants were.) A *fumbled* or dropped ball not held by either team.

loss of down — (The inability to lower yourself to your knees because you're no longer limber.) Usually results when a team receives a *penalty*. The number of downs remaining for this team then decreases when this happens.

M

man in motion — (A man who has many girlfriends and can't settle down with one.) Also known as *in motion*, this allows for one player on offense to scurry around behind the *line of scrimmage*, shifting wherever he likes to bother the defense and confuse them. However, the man who is *in motion* must, at the play's start, take one second to rest in a set position at the *line of scrimmage*. See *in motion*.

man-to-man or man-for-man — (Male bonding opportunity offering time for sports talk.) An option for a defense that has the players guarding individual players rather than zones.

marker — (Used by the kids on the walls to do artwork.) The official's way of signifying a *penalty*. The official tosses the marker, and the *referee* announces to the stadium crowd and television audience the *penalty*.

Maxwell Trophy — (Awarded for good coffee.) Presented each year to one exceptional collegiate football player.

measuring sticks — (Used to figure out sizes for your kid's clothes.) Because each *first down* is equivalent to 10 yards, there needs to be an accurate measuring device on the *field* for calculating distance, showing how much *yardage* the offense gained. Between these two *sticks*, which are kept on the sidelines, is a *chain* 10 yards long. The offensive team captain or the *referee* requests when the measuring sticks come out from the sidelines to the *field*, allowing all involved to keep track of *yardage*.

middle guard — (Protecting against increased expansion in the gut area.) This player lines up on the defensive *line*, directly across from the *center*, who plays on offense.

middle linebacker — (Protecting against increased expansion in the rear-end area.) Centered behind his defensive *line*, this player is in the heart of most action.

misdirection — (A man who mistakenly thought you were interested in dating him.) To confuse or mislead the defense, a team will have its offensive backs move together to fool the opposing squad.

monster or monster back — (A misbehaving child.) Roaming the *field*, this *linebacker* assists his teammates on defense in whatever capacity necessary to halt a *run* or thwart a *pass play*.

motion — (Handy gesticulation to send the signal that tells someone to "get lost.") Sometimes you'll hear an announcer say a man is in motion. This is when an offensive back moves back from the *line of scrimmage* or runs parallel to that line to *fake* out the other team's defense.

mousetrap — (Scattered throughout the house this implement promises to catch those varmints.) Also known as a *trap block*, this is when the offense lets an opponent blow through its offensive *line*, but then has the *guard* or *tackle block* that very defender by throwing a *block* from the side.

multiple foul — (When a child has let loose with both numbers in his diapers.) When several penalties are assessed to a team on a single *play*. In this situation, the opposition chooses the *penalty* it would like to see enforced.

multiple offense — (When a child repeatedly lets loose with both numbers in his diapers.) A situation allowing for many plays generating from a single offensive setup.

N

naked reverse — (Someone you dismiss after seeing what they look like without clothes.) An attempt by the offense to get the defense to go to one side of the *field* as the offense sends its runner to the other side to evade tacklers. To accomplish this the offense has its linemen *block* to one side, making it look as if the *play* is going that way.

National Collegiate Athletic Association — (A group of athletes who are in college.) Also known as the NCAA, this group examines all the collegiate sports happenings and supervises the management of the game, including setting rules and regulations for the organization's existence. Headquarters is in Shawnee Mission, Kansas.

National Football Conference — (Not a gathering of ladies who sell cosmetics.) This term is also known as the NFC. The *National Football League* has two conferences: the National Football Conference and the American Football Conference. At the end of the season, the two conferences play against one another in the Super Bowl, football's crown jewel, to determine the best team in the *NFL*.

National Football League — (Far different from your bowling league.) Also known as the NFL, this is the organization that each professional football team belongs to and the group that organizes game activities.

National Football League Players Association — (Something your husband would want to join.) Also known as the NFLPA, this group represents the players in their dealings with the *National Football League*.

neutral zone — (When your husband doesn't give you a "yes" or "no" to your question.) This area is a no-man's *zone*, where only the *center* on offense may go. If any player other than the *center* goes in this place—a football's expanse in width, running the length of the field—before the ball heads into *play*, this results in an encroachment *penalty* against that individual's team. The offense or defense can commit this penalty.

nickel back — (The change your kids return when you give them a $10 bill and ask them to buy a loaf of bread at the store.) The defensive back is a key component, filling in for the *linebacker* when the defensive unit decides to go with a *nickel defense*.

nickel defense — (Your kid's explanation for why the change returned from a $10 bill to buy a loaf of bread results in a nickel.) Means a team has five defensive backs on the *field*.

North-South runner — (A type of carpeting for your stairs.) A player prone to running forward during a rushing *play* as opposed to traversing the *field*.

nose man or nose tackle — (When a plastic surgeon goes to work on bettering your nose.) This defender faces off against the *center*.

number — (You wish telephone solicitors did not have yours.) Every player's jersey has a number on it to allow officials to determine who committed a *penalty* and who on offense may catch the ball. The numbering system is such that certain ranges of numbers indicate a certain position, such as quarterback or running back.

O

odd front or odd-man front or odd line — (When a vagrant hangs out in your front yard.) When the defense chooses to use a *defensive tackle* to face off against the *center* to play as if there were five players on the defensive line instead of only four.

offensive end — (A baby with diaper rash.) A team uses these players for two reasons: they are skilled at blocking, so they help runners, or they have the talent to catch passes, so they're a threat on offense. They go by the names *tight end* and *split end*. See *tight end* and *split end*.

offensive guard — (Using deodorant.) These players are skilled at wiping out defensive players, so any runner on offense has an easier chance of making it through the defenders. The offensive guards also protect their *quarterback* from an oncoming swarm of defenders. One of them lines up on each side of the *center*.

offensive tackle — (What your husband uses on fishing trips that fail to produce any fish.) Bulky men who have certain duties on offense requiring their girth. They *block* for the ballcarrier, in what many consider a thankless job. In the lineup, you can find them on the far side of each of the guards.

offensive team or offensive unit — (When your kids have not bathed.) These eleven players make up the offense and have possession of the ball.

official's time-out — (Recognizes your time off from doing chores.) Also known as a *referee's time-out*. Occurs when the *referee*, who is the top official on the *field*, asks for a *time-out* to perform a game function. In this situation, no team has a *time-out* deducted from its allowed number. During this *time-out*, frequently there is discussion of a *penalty* by the officials or, perhaps, they will ask for the yardsticks on the field to see if one team made enough *yardage* for a *first down*. See *referee's time-out*.

offside or offsides — (When you'd like to take five or ten pounds off your hips.) A five-yard *penalty* for moving past the *line of scrimmage* before the start of an offensive play.

on the numbers — (Sliding your toes over the numbers on the scale, so your mate doesn't see what you weigh.) Often said when a *pass* hits a player dead center on the jersey numbers, and that *receiver* should catch the ball.

one-back formation or one-back offense — (Thank goodness you only have one behind.) Also known as a *single-back offense*, this places a lone *back* behind the *quarterback* and the other backs as a *tight end*, *receiver*, or both.

one-on-one — (How your kids pile on each other when they wrestle.) Facing off against a single player on the opposite team.

onside kick or onsides kick — (When your husband's on the floor laying on his side and one of the kids accidentally kicks him during roughhousing.) A kick sometimes done by a team that is trailing in hopes that it will *recover* the football to score. After the ball moves forward at least 10 yards, any player on the *field* may *recover* it, unless a player on the team that isn't kicking the ball touches the ball first before it advances 10 yards. Then the kicking team must kick the ball again from a place on the field five yards back from the original spot.

open field — (What your children consider your front yard—a mini stadium for all the neighborhood kids to use.) A runner must often fend for himself in an area we call the open field, located *downfield*, because sometimes there is little blocking available for the person carrying the ball.

open-field tackle — (Roughhousing in your front yard—considered the stadium lot by the neighborhood youth.) Occurs when few defenders are available in a section of the *field* to drag down an opponent who has the ball.

option — (Should your mate buy you the mink or the tennis bracelet?) On offense, they design this play as a quarterback's choice: he may elect to do either a rushing or a *passing play*.

option clause — (If the mate buys the mink this year, the tennis bracelet will be considered next year.) Some pro football contracts have a structure with an agreement where, following the conclusion of a contract, a team may use the conditions in that contract to have the player play one more year, provided he hasn't signed with another team.

Outland Trophy — (Awarded to the pet who lands on its feet after being shoved out the door.) Given to the best collegiate player at the interior *line* position.

outlet man — (A man willing to visit the fashion outlets with you.) The defense should watch out for this man. As a receiver, he looks for a quick *pass* from the *quarterback* and helps make a reception when the main receivers have defenders hanging all over them, and the quarterback wants to unload the ball.

out of bounds — (When your children misbehave.) Beyond the end line or *sideline* and no longer considered to be in *play*.

over — (The end of a relationship.) In whatever capacity a player can muster the strength to drag his body across the *goal line* to rack up *points*.

overload — (Five different dates in five nights.) Flooding a part of the *field* with members from the offense, making the defense panic because they don't have sufficient players to defend against a *play* there.

overplay — (When you call your children in from outside for a meal.) A strategy designed to make an opponent use his weaker side by guarding his stronger area.

overshift — (When you wish your weight would be redistributed.) Practiced by the defense to get their largest playmakers to the ball, this involves moving some men on the defensive *line* to the *strong side* of that defensive *line*.

overthrow — (Telling your kids they can't go out when their father has said they can.) Passing beyond the offensive *receiver*, so far away the player is unable to catch the *pass*.

overtime — (You hope you will acquire more diamonds during this period.) For competition that remains in a tie after all game time has expired, the game lasts another 15 minutes, concluding when one team heads into the *end zone* for a *touchdown* or kicks a *field goal* or scores a *safety*, or when time expires.

P

pass — (When a waiter delivers a drink to your table from a man you don't know.) A throw moving the ball forward.

pass action — (Accepting the drink from the man you don't know who had the waiter deliver it to your table.) When a *quarterback drops back* a few steps from the *line of scrimmage* as if he were going to *pass* the ball and, instead, he hands the ball to a running back for a carry. The quarterback tries to deceive the other team, which may result in some needed *yardage* for his team.

pass-completion average — (The ratio of women who accept a man's flirtatious gesture.) Taking a *quarterback's* number of *pass* completions and dividing that by the number of thrown passes gives us this *statistic*. We have an indication of how good the *quarterback* is after knowing this number, though the statistic doesn't reflect if his *receivers* dropped any catchable passes.

pass defense — (Having an excuse ready for a man you don't know who had a waiter deliver a drink to your table.) Required of the *linebackers* and *secondary*, who will cover potential *receivers* as those *receivers* head *downfield* on their *pass routes*.

pass drop — (When a flirtatious gesture fails.) When a *quarterback* on offense retreats from the *line of scrimmage* to scan the *field* for one of his men *downfield* who can catch the ball he's about to heave.

pass interference — (When a man you don't know asks the waiter to send you a drink and the waiter delivers that beverage to the wrong table.) Considered unfair *play* when a defender affects a *receiver's* ability to haul in a *pass* tossed *downfield*.

pass pattern — (When a man repeatedly makes flirtatious gestures.) Moves by the *pass* catchers on offense. This requires *pass receivers* running in a set fashion that the *quarterback* predetermines in the *huddle*, so he knows where to throw the ball.

pass play — (Acting coy after a man's flirtatious gesture.) A *play* involving a throw to move the ball forward.

pass protection — (Having a friend with you to potentially deflect an unwanted pass from a man you don't know.) Hustling to defend the player throwing the ball, so he has no outside *interference* hampering the *pass play*.

pass receiver — (The recipient of the flirtatious gesture.) A player who catches the ball as it heads forward, and is eligible to do so. This means if you *play* as a *back* or an *end* on offense, you can be a pass receiver.

pass route — (The path on which a flirtatious gesture from a man travels.) Planned in the offensive *huddle* and assigned by the *quarterback*, these designed plans indicate how *receivers* will *run*, so the *quarterback* will always have a sense of where his players are before completing a *pass play*.

pass rush — (When a man's in a hurry to make a flirtatious gesture.) Having the defenders on the *line* come after the *quarterback* and try to *tackle* him.

passing down — (Rejecting a man's flirtatious gesture.) If a team requires substantial *yardage*, or if a *run* just won't cut it, a broadcaster might refer to the *play* as a passing down, indicating the critical nature of the *pass* to get a new set of *downs*.

PAT — (A woman's name.) *Point after touchdown.* Could be one *point* (for a kick) or two (for a *pass*). See *point after touchdown*.

pattern — (What you use when you sew.) A *quarterback* and his teammates discuss in the *huddle* where a *receiver* will end up *downfield*, so the *pass* may go there, and the *receiver* can run to it and catch it.

penalty — (What the kids face when they misbehave.) A rules violation resulting in a loss of *yardage* from five to 15 yards.

penalty flag or penalty marker — (Ways to signal when your kids have done something wrong.) When someone violates the rules, any official may grab his own yellow handkerchief and toss it out ·on the playing *field*. This action notifies the players that someone has done something to break the game rules.

penetration — (When the detergent gets the collar of the shirt clean.) You can use this term one of two ways. First, if a team's defense is porous and the offense crashes through it at will, the team is said to make penetration. Second, if the defensive *line* makes mincemeat of its opponents, that offensive *line* may be easily penetrated.

period — (A form of punctuation.) Also known as *quarters*, there are four of these, 15 minutes in length, during one game. See *quarters*.

personal foul — (When someone tells you about your bad breath.) A 15-yard *penalty* for conduct on the *field* considered hazardous or not in the spirit of the game.

pick up the blitz — (Keeping things off your house's floor.) Requires reading the defense and expecting the opponent to charge forward toward the offense. The offense must then make wholesale changes to protect their team and the ball.

piling on — (Refers to something on carpet.) A 15-yard *penalty* for leaping onto a player after he is *down*.

pitchout — (Done to old food in the refrigerator.) Done by the *quarterback* to get the ball to a running back by throwing it underhanded behind the *line of scrimmage*.

placekick — (Enjoying where you live.) Happens at the beginning of the game or following a *touchdown* or *field goal*. This also comes into *play* when a team attempts a *field goal* or *extra-point conversion*. The offense will use this method of placing the ball on the ground with someone holding it to kick for some *points*.

platoon — (Feeding your kids and the neighbors.) When all eleven players come into the game at one time and make up the entire offense or the whole defense for one particular team.

play — (What your children want to do in the dining room, when the fine china's on the table and the crystal's out.) Plays often relate to the particular strengths of a team, its *field* position, and other variables, such as the time remaining in a game and the score of the game. All teammates are versed in the plays because the offense and defense, separately and together, *run* them in practice.

play-action fake — (When the children say they'll go outside, but stay inside and roughhouse.) The *quarterback* pretends to give the ball to a running back on offense, and then, the *quarterback* throws the ball to a *receiver downfield*.

play-action pass — The *quarterback* pretends to have a *running play* in mind by deceiving the other team with a *handoff* that never happens. Instead, he tosses the ball *downfield*.

playbook — Designed to be a guide of how each play works. The coaches draft these ideas and give them to players during practice drills in spring camp.

play-by-play — (When your children are outside playing, and the neighbor's children on both sides of your house are out playing.) Done by analysts in a broadcast booth or on the *sidelines* for a radio or television audience. This information for the audience includes a narration of what's happening on the *field*.

plunge — (Motion used to clear your toilet when plugged up.) Moving forward at full strength on a *running play* or when close to the *end zone*, using force to rack up a few yards.

pocket — (Where you find discarded bubble gum, candy wrappers, and crayons once pants make their way into the clothes hamper.) A launching pad for the *quarterback*, who uses this area to scan the *field*, find open *receivers*, and fire the football *downfield*, provided the *quarterback's* blockers shelter this territory. An area where teammates attempt to protect their *quarterback*, so he can find open *receivers*. See *pocket passer*.

pocket passer — Faced with an onslaught of opponents ready to pester him, often the *quarterback* will throw from a secure area protected by his teammates, a few steps back from the *line of scrimmage*, giving the *quarterback* time to get a *play* going. See *pocket*.

points — (A man earns these if he treats you well.) A team collects points on this scale each time it scores: *point-after touchdown* or *extra point*, 1; two-point *conversion* following a *touchdown*, 2; *safety*, 2; *field goal*, 3; *touchdown*, 6.

point after touchdown — Some refer to this as an *extra point* or *conversion*. Concerning conversions, this is an opportunity for a team to earn two *points* by getting the ball into the *end zone* on the ground or in the air in one *play* following a *touchdown*. Or, in a second option, known as an *extra point*, this awards one *point* to a team if it kicks the ball through the *uprights* of the *goalposts*. See *PAT*.

point spread — This is a way of determining which is the better of two teams and noting this by assigning *points* to the superior team, indicating how many *points* by which they will win a game. Oddsmakers are responsible for choosing who will win and by how much.

possession — (Makeup, clothes, jewelry.) Regulating the action on the *field* by having the ball. Total time of possession is important and shows up in game *statistics* because an opponent can't score when it does not have the ball.

possession football — (When your husband has the television remote during football season.) When the offense holds onto the football by systematically plotting *run* after *run*, and when throwing, doing so on high-percentage short *passes*.

post — (Part of a pierced earring.) Involves an offensive *pass* catcher sprinting full-speed ahead, then splitting paths from that *pattern* to head toward the *field's* middle and near the location of the *goalposts*.

post blocking — Making it tough on a defender, a player on offense will *drive* his opponent away from his secure spot on the *line of scrimmage* while a second player goes up and spins the defender around like a top.

pour it on — (Throwing salad dressing on the salad just before your company comes.) Crushing an opposing team by scoring an unnecessary number of *points* to defeat it.

power block — The offensive linemen will push away the defensive linemen, thrusting them to the *sidelines* or rearward, so that the running back can burst through the open *holes* in the offensive *line*.

power I — When a team operates with three running backs lined up in the backfield behind the *quarterback*.

power play — The wish of every runner. Designed to emphasize the brute strength of blockers, who form a wall around the runner, enabling him to gain *yardage* when the blockers mow down defenders directly in the path of their runner.

power sweep — (A vacuum cleaner.) Employing the *guard* on the offensive *line* to *drop back* and guide his teammate, who has the ball, to the extreme end of their team's *formation*.

prayer — (What you say just before reviewing your kid's report card.) Also known as a *Hail Mary* pass, and done in desperation, this toss goes *downfield*, often into a crowd, with a slim chance of someone catching it. See *Hail Mary*.

pressure — Making the opposition's *quarterback* get rid of the ball hurriedly, therefore, often resulting in a bad *play*. Another use of this term includes when the players on offense want to make room for their runner, so they consistently try to push aside and move defenders away from the ballcarrier.

prevent defense — (Babyproofing your house before your friends with a two-year-old and a three-year-old come over to visit.) A strategy by the defense to yield a short *running play* or a dinky *pass play* for little *yardage*, while fiercely defending against a long *pass* by bringing in an extra person to protect against that *pass*. That player will play as a defensive back or a *linebacker*.

Pro Football Hall of Fame — This museum in Canton, Ohio, recognizes owners and athletes noted as the finest in pro football. Those featured in the museum received a nod from the fans to go on a ballot and were elected by media types.

pro set — (Setting the table expertly.) On offense, this has the resemblance to a "T," with the *quarterback* in the *backfield*, and a *split end* on one side of him and a *wide receiver* on the other side.

protect a player — When a team wants to make sure no other gets to take a player from their lineup during a special *draft*, for instance, when the Baltimore Ravens came into the league and they had to have players. A team can protect a player by several strategies, so he's spared from the *draft*.

pulling guard — (A lifeguard who just pulled your kid out of a tidal wave.) Involves a *guard* with the responsibility of blocking for the runner, who would like to make his way toward the *sideline*, so he can run *downfield* from that vantage point.

punt — (What you do when the baby's hollering, the electricity's out, and your only car—with your husband in it—broke down on the highway.) When a team kicks the ball *downfield* after it fails to gain a *first down*.

punt formation — On offense, this *formation* has the punting, or kicking the ball, occur from a point some 15 yards or so in back of the *line of scrimmage*.

punt return — After a team kicks, or *punts* the ball to the other team, an opposing player takes the ball and runs *upfield* as far as he can go.

punt-return specialist — Relying on someone with elusive moves and an ability to sprint to catch a *punt* and run it *upfield*. Typically, this player will be part of a *special-teams* unit; however, some squads will bring in a *receiver* or running back because of their ball-handling ability.

put it up — Throwing the football to a teammate.

Q

quarterback — (Change returned from your child after sending him out with a fifty-dollar bill to buy the newspaper.) The team leader on offense who calls the *plays*, although sometimes the coach prescribes the *plays*. The quarterback throws *passes* to his teammates or can hand the ball off to them, or he can *run* with the ball from his position in the middle of the lineup, behind the *center*.

quarterback sneak — This *play's* purpose is to gain short *yardage* or a *touchdown* by having the quarterback take the *handoff* directly from the *center* and *plunging* quickly ahead. See *sneak*.

quarters — (What you believe is a fair allowance rate for your teen-age children.) This is the same definition as *periods*. There are four in a game. Each is 15 minutes. See *periods*.

quick count — (Lining the children up at the door and counting them as they head out the door for school to be sure all catch the school bus.) Relying on the *quarterback*, this strategy calls for him to abbreviate his *signal* count to take the opposition off guard and get them rattled.

quick hitter — A fast-developing play on offense emphasizing the ability of the runner to take the ball quickly through a gap of defenders created by the blockers on offense.

quick kick — (The speed of your children when they exchange kicks in the back seat of the car, but you don't see them in the act.) Typically, a team on offense *punts* on *fourth down*; however, a *punt* on any other *down* usually dumbfounds the defense and gives the offense an advantage.

quick opener — Leaving little to the imagination, this play involves the *quarterback* giving the ball to a running back in his belly and having him run full-steam ahead with no excess showmanship.

quick out — (The time from when you give your child a beverage to the time it's poured on the kitchen floor.) Relying on speed and precision for its successful execution, this has a *receiver* dashing *downfield* a few yards and then sharply veering toward the *sideline* for the swift *pass* from the *quarterback*.

quick release — Usually said of a *quarterback* when he can *drop back*, aim for a *receiver*, and quickly and accurately toss a sharp *pass*.

quick slant — (What happens to the food on your child's highchair, once he lifts the tray.) This *play* involves the *quarterback* giving the ball to a running back in his belly and having him run at a *slant* toward the *line* of defenders ahead of him.

R

read — Sizing up and correctly assuming what a defensive or offensive unit will do and how they will react when a *play* is going on.

reach block — Keeping the defender at bay, the offensive line works to restrain the defensive linemen, keeping them in the *center*, rather than toward the *sidelines* or the outside of the *field*.

reach-and-wheel blocking — A bit of trickery by the offense, which has its linemen allow the defense to get past them, only to swing them out of the play's flow and into a position where they're helpless and useless to the defense.

receive — (To get something, say a dozen red roses.) Grabbing a *pass* or taking control of a kicked ball, such as after a *punt* or *kickoff*.

receiver — (Not a stereo component.) Someone eligible to catch a thrown or a kicked football.

receiving team — Denotes the squad ready to catch a *punt* or *kickoff*.

recover — (Finding that lost earring behind the sofa cushion.) When there is a *fumble*, or someone drops a ball when fielding it, and another person picks it up.

recruiting — (Convincing one of your girlfriends to come with you on a blind date.) Persuading accomplished high-school football players to enroll at a university to participate on that college's football squad.

red-dog — Also known as a *blitz*, this is when the defensive backs and *linebackers* charge into the *line* to try to *tackle* the *quarterback*, typically on a *passing play*. See *blitz* and *shoot*.

redshirt — (What happens when you put your white shirt in the washing machine with the bright colors.) An extra year for a college football player to learn more about the game or recuperate from past injuries while not using any of his four years of collegiate athletic eligibility because he is not considered a part of the team as a redshirt.

red zone — Plays executed by the offense that are from the defense's 10-yard line or even closer to the *goal line*.

referee — The head official who gets the game going, supervising each *play's* start time and the action on the *field*, including rule infractions by the offense and violations of the rights of kickers and passers. He also is on the lookout for *lateral passes*.

referee's time-out — Also known as an *official's time-out*. Occurs when the *referee*, who is the top official on the *field*, asks for a *time-out* to perform a game function. In this situation, neither team has a *time-out* charged to its side. During this *time-out*, frequently there is discussion by the officials of a *penalty* or, perhaps, the officials will ask for the *yardsticks* to come out to see if one team made enough *yardage* for a *first down*. See *official's time-out*.

refusal of penalties — This is when a team *declines a penalty* called against the other team. After some consideration, it may be more advantageous for one team to have the opponent's *downs* advanced, rather than having *yardage* assessed against that team because it had a *penalty*.

regular — (One of the neighborhood kids, who routinely shows up for dinner.) Not a backup player, but an individual who typically appears in a lineup.

replay — When the cameras catch on videotape a *down* or action of interest and play it again for the fans on TV. Likewise, there are stadiums with large screens at the game itself capable of showing featured happenings again.

reserve — (Someone you have in mind to take to the wedding as a date if your first choice can't make it.) A person, who does not typically start a game, but comes in as a backup.

return — (Something you do with a wedding gift you don't like.) Forward movement following the catch of an *interception*, *punt*, or *kickoff*.

return men — Players specializing in taking the ball *upfield* once the opponents boot it from a *kickoff* or *punt*. These runners try to advance the ball as close to the other team's *end zone* as possible.

returner — A player who brings back a *punt* or kick or runs *upfield* after making an *interception*.

reverse — (Changing at the last minute the outfit you plan to wear on a date.) Occurring in the *backfield* on offense, one running back has the ball and runs in one uninterrupted path parallel with the *line of scrimmage*, meeting up with another running back sprinting the opposite way, but parallel to the line of scrimmage, to whom he hands the ball, thoroughly confusing the defense.

rollout — (Taking the rolls out of the oven.) Requires the mobility of the *quarterback* on offense to move out of the *pocket* formed by blockers and to head toward one side of the *field* to gain a better vantage point to throw the ball or *run* with it.

rotation — Shifting players about to compensate for weaknesses in the defense when no one is in a particular region and someone needs to *guard* that area.

roughing the kicker — A 15-yard *penalty* from the spot of the infraction. This occurs when the kicker, rather than the ball he's trying to boot *downfield*, gets knocked down or hit by a defender first. Punters are particularly vulnerable to injury if they are hit while in the act of kicking.

roughing the passer — A 15-yard *penalty* from the spot of the infraction. This occurs when the *quarterback* gets knocked down or hit after he has already thrown a *pass downfield*.

route — (Your son has one of these; he delivers papers.) A certain path a *receiver* follows to catch the ball from the *quarterback*.

Rozelle Rule — A player leaving a team following his option year who is now a *free agent*. Under league rules, the team he goes to for the upcoming season must pay some type of compensation to the team from which he departed.

run — (Not a tear in your panty hose.) Moving the ball on the ground rather than in the air.

runback — Taking the ball *downfield* after an *interception*, or following a kick or *punt*.

running game — Relying on a strategy of *rushing* to gain *yardage* instead of throwing *passes*.

running lanes — Ten fictitious *holes* spreading widthwise across the *field* used for running plays on offense.

running play — Known frequently as a *rushing play*, this means taking the ball *upfield* on the ground as opposed to the air.

run off blockers — The running back in this *play*, and in this offense, relies on his offensive blockers to open a *hole* for him to run through. In the offensive *huddle*, the *play* called determines the *hole* the running back should go through. Try as it may, sometimes the blockers have zero luck blasting a path for the running back to run through. In this case, the running back has to use his own dynamite to navigate through.

run out the clock — Keeping the ball on offense by using every available second on the play clock and trying to keep the ball *inbounds* to consume game time.

run pursuit — (Trying to apply nail polish to the run in your panty hose.) During a *running play* by the offense, the defense reacts by containing the runner, filling any *holes*, and maintaining backup strength to *tackle* the ballcarrier in case he bursts through an earlier line of defenders.

run to daylight — (A run you don't discover until the next morning of your date.) Thrown to the wolves? Nah. This strategy has the ballcarrier going full-speed ahead to any break in the *line* where he can fit his body and wiggle between defenders. Of course, the offensive *line* does its best to provide *holes* big enough through which to send yachts.

rush — (In a hurry to get out of the house to meet your date.) A running *play* on offense, or to hurry a *quarterback* or kicker to thwart a successful throw, *punt*, or kick.

S

sack — (Holds potatoes.) Requires a defender to toss a *quarterback* to the ground before he crosses the *line of scrimmage, completes* a reception to a teammate, or hands the ball off to a teammate.

safety — If the defense manages to grab the ballcarrier on offense in his own *end zone*, the defense gets two *points* added to its score.

safetyman — You can use this definition in one of two ways. First, this might be a defender whose role is to *guard* against *pass plays* or runs far *downfield*. A second usage refers to the person who catches the ball when a team *punts* or kicks it. Standing behind everyone else, he fields the kick and tears *upfield*.

safety sack — When a *safety* causes a *sack*.

safety valve — (A backup baby-sitter, in case your regular one cancels.) Many times, the *quarterback* will look to his *receivers downfield* to catch a *pass*. If they are covered, he'll dump the ball off to a running back who is close by to avoid an onslaught of defenders who want to *tackle* him.

scissors — (Useful for snipping bangs.) Also known as a *cross block*. On offense, a *tackler* will hit a defender at a sideways angle instead of meeting him face to face. See *cross block*.

scout — (You're a den mother.) Teams have personnel who determine the skill level of athletes whom they may want to acquire in a *draft* or through a trade. This also means a coach or players take a look at another team during play to examine their methods, and then design an offense and a defense to match up against that opponent.

scramble block — Similar to imitating an animal, this block has the blockers on offense put their hands and knees on the ground, sacrificing their bodies as human roadblocks in the paths of the oncoming defense.

scrape — Happens on defense and involves appearing in time to bolt through the *front line* in a *hole* created by another defensive player in the *line*.

scrimmage — Pits two teams in competition against one another to simulate game situations, only the players on the *field* are all teammates.

scrimmage kick — Football rules consider *field-goal* tries and *punts* scrimmage kicks rather than *free kicks* because scrimmage kicks start when the *center hikes* the ball from the *line of scrimmage*, they allow for the possibility of a *blocked* kick, and the ball must travel a certain distance before the kicking squad can go after it.

seam — (Has to do with your dress.) When a team uses a *zone* defense sometimes it will leave some space from part of one *zone* to another.

seam route — Also known as a *shoot route*. A team uses a running back on this *pass play* to run a short sprint straight ahead, twisting backward to catch the short dump from the *quarterback*, as the running back *splits a seam* between *zones* in the defense. See *shoot route*.

second and long — (A long day on the second day of the month.) Refers to a situation where it's second *down* and the offense must travel at least seven yards to gain a *first down*.

second and medium — Refers to a situation where it's second *down* and the offense must travel between three to six yards to gain a *first down*.

second and short — Refers to a situation where it's second *down* and the offense must travel two or fewer yards to gain a *first down*.

secondary — (Not as important—an old boyfriend, for example.) Considered the players on defense who are the *safeties* and *cornerbacks*.

secondary receiver — (A backup boyfriend.) A player on offense who the *quarterback* considers the second choice to throw the ball to if he can't get the ball to his first choice.

series — (Television sitcom.) Applies to an offensive squad given four opportunities to head *downfield* 10 yards.

set back — (When your boyfriend dumps you.) A player on offense, typically a running back, such as a *halfback* or *fullback*, who sets up behind the *quarterback*.

shank — (You discuss this with your butcher in the meat portion of the store.) If the kicker doesn't connect with the ball correctly—for instance if he hits anywhere but on his instep—the ball goes off at an angle and the players call it a shank.

shift — (Moving a date from one night to the next.)   A strategy designed to confuse the defense when some of the offensive players move from their positions after maintaining their position for a one-second count before the *center hikes* the ball.

shoestring tackle — When a defender hauls down the opposing team's ballcarrier by latching on to his foot, twisting him to the ground.

shoot — (What you say when you don't have a key ingredient to make tonight's dinner.) Also known as *blitz* and *red-dog*. Involves a *safety* or *linebacker* coming in and trying to *tackle* the person on offense tossing the ball. See *blitz* and *red-dog*.

shoot route — Also known as a *seam route*. A team uses a running back on this *pass play* to run a short sprint straight ahead, twisting backward to catch the short dump from the *quarterback*, as the running back *splits a seam* between *zones* in the defense. See *seam route*.

shoot the gap — Tossing aside men on the offensive *line* to grab the person on offense with the ball.

shootout — The scoring of many *points*, resulting in a lopsided contest between two teams.

short side — Also known as *weak side*.   Identifies a situation where there are fewer players on one side of the *line* than the other side. See *weak side*.

short-yardage offense — Bulking up and adding more of the big players in front, who normally play as offensive linemen, with the idea it will be easier to gain access to the *end zone* or move forward for a *first down* if there are more big men to lead the way.

shotgun — A real clue a team will *pass* because the *quarterback* starts the play on offense lined up about seven yards behind his *center*, giving him time to size up the developing *play*.

shoulder tackle — Method of *tackling* involving propelling the full force of a *tackler's* shoulder into the chest of an opposing ballcarrier. To increase the pain, the defender goes after the legs, wrapping his arms around them to bring the carrier down.

shovel pass — (Handing the shovel to your mate for use in the garden.) Used by the offense and simulating the motion of a person using a shovel to scoop dirt from a trench. This frequently is the method of completing *laterals* or *pitchouts*, but not *forward passes*, which travel overhand.

shuffle — (Done with a deck of cards.) Used to keep up with an opponent. This foot movement has a player drag one foot in a certain direction, with the other foot moved to the same point.

side judge — As one of the officials, he lines up *downfield* to observe things, such as the movement of the ball, determining when it heads *out of bounds*. Other areas for him to concentrate on include the following: determining the legitimacy of a *field goal* or a two-point play; tracking the number of *time-outs*; making sure there aren't too many defenders on the field on any one play; and deciding when *clipping* and *pass interference* occur.

sideline — (An extra job.) An indicator used by the officials to tell when someone is *out of bounds*. These lines are at the sides of the playing *field* and connect to the *goal line* and *end line*. The term also refers to a *pass pattern* involving a sprint straight ahead by the offensive pass catcher, who breaks his sprint to jerk to the sideline where, if conducted successfully, the *pass* reaches his hands, giving him the option of stepping *out of bounds* or spinning the opposite way to gain additional *yardage* on a continued *run*.

sideline pattern or sideline route — Used for clock-management purposes to stretch out the remaining time as a game winds down. This has the *pass* catcher on offense running *downfield* and then cutting toward the *sideline* to step *out of bounds* and stop the clock just after he makes the reception.

sidewinder — A type of snake, and you hate snakes.) Also known as a *soccer-style kicker*, who comes at the ball from an angle instead of straight ahead, preferring to boot the ball with the instep. See *soccer-style kicker*.

signals — (Control traffic.) Used by the *quarterback* to guide his teammates on an offensive *play*. These noises or words let the teammates know specifics of the *play*, if changed from the *huddle*. Typically, if the *play* does not change from the one planned in the *huddle*, the signals indicate when the *quarterback* will receive the *hike* of the ball from the *center*.

single-back offense — Also known as a *one-back formation, one-back offense*. Has the running back positioned in the *backfield* in a line with the *quarterback* with other running backs fanning out to play in the place of other *receivers*, such as the *wide receiver* or the *tight end*.

sixty-minute player — An athlete with incredible energy and versatility capable of playing the whole length of the game as part of the offensive and defensive units. Seldom seen today, at the pro or college level, with the great specialization of players. See *two-way player*.

skull practice — See *chalk talk* or *skull session*.

skull session — Also known as *chalk talk* or *skull practice*. This is when a team gets together off the *field* and talks about an upcoming or a past game and how to defend against certain plays or what the team will do in the next contest. A coach leads these sessions.

slant — This play has the person with the ball on offense run forward in a way that has him *rushing* at an angle.

slant-in — When the *pass* catcher moves forward at an angle to approach the *end zone* to be in position to catch the ball.

slant route — Has the *defensive ends* and *defensive tackles* trying to get through the *line* set up by the offense by turning their bodies at an angle, allowing the defenders to slither through.

slasher — (A vandal piercing car tires with a knife.) A running style emphasizing bulling through the middle of the *field* rather than sprinting and twisting past defenders.

sleeper play — (Playing in your pajamas.) Also known as a *hideout play* and *dead-man play*. No longer allowed in the *NFL*, this play had some trickery involved. It involved a player heading toward the *sidelines*—as if another offensive player were to replace him—and then he hovered just *inbounds*, suddenly sprinting *downfield* when the play began. See *hideout play* and *dead-man play*.

slingshot goalposts — Used by professionals, this is a *goalpost* with just one pole in the ground rather than the two *goalposts* in the ground favored by those on the high school or collegiate level.

slotback — (Has to do with the Las Vegas gambling scene.) This player fits into the lineup on offense when he positions himself in the space between an *end* and a *tackle*.

snap — When the *center* on offense starts the *play* by moving the ball from the ground between his legs to an awaiting teammate behind him, usually the *quarterback* or a kicker.

snap count — (Counting to ten before you hurl angry remarks at your mate.) A *quarterback* uses this to tell his teammates how the *play* will progress and when to expect the *snap* of the ball from *center*. A defense might use it to specify a certain *alignment* for a particular *play*.

snapper — The player who *hikes* the ball to the *quarterback*.

sneak — (Eating dessert before dinner.) Also known as a *quarterback sneak*. This play's purpose is to gain safe and sure short *yardage* or a *touchdown* by having the quarterback take the *handoff* directly from the *center* and plunging quickly ahead. See *quarterback sneak*.

soccer-style kicker — Also known as a *sidewinder*, who comes at the ball from an angle instead of straight ahead, preferring to boot the ball with the instep. See *sidewinder*.

soft — (A type of contact lens.) Occurs when a player on defense gives some space to the player on offense he has the responsibility to cover.

solid play — (When your kids play for at least an hour without interrupting you.) The offense is sly enough to disguise its play tactics so the defense can't figure out what will happen next. In its *formation*, the offense doesn't give any indication of what it will do, leaving the defense guessing.

spear — A foul for using a helmet as a weapon on the *field* by burying it in a competitor's stomach and chest areas.

special team — Also known as the *suicide squad* or *bomb squad*, this group of players comes on the *field* during situations where there's a *punt*, a *kickoff*, or a *field-goal* condition. They have special skills, such as speed or kicking ability. See *suicide squad* or *bomb squad*.

spike — (The name of the tow-truck driver you got your car from this morning.) Usually you'll see a player do this as a way to celebrate a score he made. It involves throwing the ball to the ground in the *end zone.*

spinout — A runner's method of getting away from defenders by turning sharply, jarring a defender's hold.

spinner play — Aimed at faking out the defense. Hiking the ball to the *fullback* and using him as a decoy, the fullback twirls completely around, doing a good job of acting as he makes fake *handoffs* or gives the ball to his running-back teammates.

split end — (Signifies a problem with your hair.) Responsible for catching passes, this player takes his position on the outside of the offensive *formation.* See *flanker, wide receiver, spread end, offensive end,* and *tight end.*

split the seam — When the *quarterback* throws the football to a spot *downfield,* so that it goes to an open area in the center of the *field* where there are no defenders.

spot — (Usually ruins your best blouse.) A decision the officials make indicating where the ball rests before the next *play* begins.

spot of foul — When an official can call a *penalty* based on where it happened and have the next *play* take place from that particular *spot.*

spot of enforcement — Indicates where a *penalty* happened and from where the officials will subtract *penalty yardage.*

spot pass — A timing *play* where a *quarterback* on offense throws the ball to a location decided in advance. If all goes as planned, the teammate catches it there.

spread end — Also known as *split end, flanker,* or *wide receiver,* this player catches passes and lines up at the far end of the offensive *formation.* See *split end, flanker,* or *wide receiver.*

spread formation — In this *formation* on offense, the running backs position themselves so they are widely spread out in the *backfield.*

spread set — When you're watching a game—whether in the stands or at your home—watch for a *play* where the running backs line up far from where they normally position themselves. Because the *backs* are so far apart, there is little likelihood of them blocking for each other, thus signaling a probable *pass* to the defense.

spying — (Checking in on who your kids are talking to on the phone.) Being patient and watching the *play* develop before committing to a defensive *rush*.

square-in — An offensive *play* where the *pass* catcher runs a *route* that takes him forward and has him dart inside toward the middle of the field and head to the other *sideline*.

square-out — (When you dump the nerd who asked you out previously.) An offensive *play* where the *pass* catcher runs a *route* that takes him forward and then has him run toward the outside of the field and head to the nearest *sideline*.

squeeze — (Used to rate freshness of bread.) A tactic where the offense concentrates on a member of the defensive *line* by covering him with two men.

stack — (Piled up bills.) Used by the offense to keep the defense in the dark about a developing *play's* direction. When a group of players clump together, the defense gets confused about where they'll head.

stand one up — (Not showing for a date you made with a man.) Making the necessary moves to get a player to a place where he cannot move ahead from his upright location.

stashing — Not allowed in the *National Football League*. A team might have a star player it would like to keep on the roster. To do so, the team may call a player hurt, adding him to the injured reserve list when, in reality, he isn't injured. This action is unlawful, and if discovered by league officials, it results in monetary punishment and league penalties.

statistics — Widely used for comparisons, box scores, and game summaries, these numbers give us measures to determine the effectiveness of a team's offense and defense.

Statue of Liberty play — (Symbol of freedom.) Done by the offense by positioning someone in the *backfield*, who holds the ball in the air and imitates the throwing motion, while another player from the same team takes the ball from the outstretched player's arm to *run* with it.

steal — (A bargain.) A move that results in a player losing the football because an opponent scuffled with him and jarred the ball loose. Considered within the rules. See *strip*.

sticks — (Someone who lives in an undesirable part of town.) Also known as a *chain*, this is the measurement instrument 10 yards long that is used to gauge when a team achieves a *first down*. See *yardage chain* or *chain*.

stone hands — (Happens when you don't wear gloves to wash dishes.) Refers to someone who can't hold onto a football after the *quarterback* tosses it or after someone *punts* it.

stop and go — A deceptive move executed by a pass catcher when he sprints forward, *fakes* a catch not long after running forward, only to pour it on and *run* straight ahead expecting the *quarterback* to throw it to him further *downfield*.

stopping the clock — (Method to prevent aging.) The clock stops when a *pass* catcher, who has made a reception, steps *out of bounds* while he has the ball. The clock also halts when the offense tosses an *incomplete pass*. Because of these rules, a team wanting to catch up in the closing minutes of a game will use the *pass play* to their advantage.

straight-arm — A measure used by a runner to escape an oncoming tackler. It involves a runner extending his arm fully and raising his hand to push an opponent away.

stretch a zone — (Trying to fit into a size 10 when you wear a size 14.) Looking *downfield*, the offense will get off a throw to an awaiting *pass* catcher near the *sideline* to avoid a defender in a *zone* defense.

strip — A method of forcing an opponent to *fumble* the football by poking or jerking at the ball, so that the opponent loses control.

strong safety — When a *safety* positions himself crosswise from the offensive *line's strong side*.

strong side — (Has nothing to do with weightlifting ability.) A feature of a *line* if it has more players on one side than the other. The side with more players is the strong side.

stunt — Movement by the defense to get the beefy men on the offensive *line* upset. The defenders move back and forth at the *line of scrimmage*, hoping to throw off the offensive *line*.

stutter step — To elude a defender by pretending to go one way, and then going the opposite, leaving the defender grasping at air. A tactic used by the ballcarrier or *receiver* to get the defender to commit himself to moving in one direction.

sucker block — (Preventing lollipop affixment to the car seat by advance anticipation of such a move.) Used by a lineman on offense as a device to get the opposition faked out and unable to make a *play*.

sucker trap — Also known as a *false trap*, this has the offensive lineman trying to *fake* out his opponent by blocking one way, trying to get the defender to follow him, while the runner goes through the empty hole where the defender once was. See *false trap*.

suicide squad — Also known as the *special team* or *bomb squad*, this group of players comes on the *field* during situations where there's a *punt*, a *kickoff*, or a *field-goal* condition. These are players with special skills, such as speed or kicking ability. See *special team* or *bomb squad*.

sweep — (Household chore.) By having his teammates form a protective shield around him, the ballcarrier sprints to the end of the *formation*, where these blockers lead the way for, what a team hopes, is a big *gain* in *yardage*.

swing pass — Done on offense, this is a simple toss meant for one of the running backs who heads toward the *sideline*.

T

T formation — (A way to arrange your tea party.) Looks like the letter "T" on the *field* if you were to see this *formation* from an aerial photo taken above the *field*. You would observe the *fullback* directly behind the *quarterback*, with his fellow running backs—the *halfbacks*—flanking him, but several yards apart from the *fullback*.

tackle — (Something your mate uses on his fishing trips.) Three meanings to this word, two referring to positions on the *field* and a third relating to an action on the *field*. One of the positions is on offense, the other on defense. The two *defensive tackles* situate themselves inside the *defensive ends*, and have as their duties going after the *quarterback* and stopping the *rush* when it heads to the inner part of the *field*. There are two of these *ends*.

The *offensive tackles* place themselves on the outside shoulders of the two *guards*, who are part of the offensive *line*. As dual goals, they want to make sure their *quarterback* has time to throw the ball or, if it's a *running play*, that their ballcarrier has room to *run* because they blasted opponents out of the way, so the runner could make it through the *front line* easily.

The final definition for this word means when a player goes after his opponent with the intent of dragging him to the ground, so he can't advance the ball.

tailback — A player on offense whose job it is to *run* with the ball, catch *passes*, and *block*. His position entails that he line up in the *backfield*—the greatest distance from the *quarterback* if he is in a *formation*, such as the "*I.*"

taxi squad — (A group that takes you from the bar if you've had too much to drink.) These players are members of a football team. These athletes practice, but can't play in any league competitions.

TD — (Short for "to do.") A *touchdown* worth six points. See *touchdown*.

tear-away jersey — (Your mate wonders if Victoria's Secret sells this.) A shirt made for use by some players on offense, specifically running backs and *pass* catchers, who want to elude the defenders' tight grip.

telegraph — (Sending your mate a message that a dozen red roses would be nice.) Unintentionally signaling the other team as to what might happen on a *pass play* or a *run* from *scrimmage*.

thread the needle — (Basis for sewing anything.) A precise throw from a *quarterback*, who tosses the football to a *receiver* with defenders near him.

three and out — Just like in baseball, where the team out in the *field* hopes three batters come up to the plate and make three consecutive outs, allowing the defenders to come to the plate, the defense in football wants little *yardage* to be made on the first three *downs* by the offense, making the fourth *down* so far away from the *down* markers as to be unachievable by the offense, halting the offense's *possession*.

three-end offense — When the *wide receiver, tight end,* and *split end* play on the *field* in one offensive *alignment*.

three-man front — When a team uses two *defensive ends* and a nose guard on defense.

three-point stance — Basic position learned early on in the set of football skills. This involves the player placing his hand on the ground with his legs separated by some distance. He assumes a bent position with his butt in the air, while most of his weight rests on his hand. You'll see this position taken at the start of plays.

throw a strike — (A bad date.) A football tossed with such precision as to be easily catchable, resulting in a reception.

throw into traffic — (To hit rush hour.) A ball that has a greater chance of being *intercepted* by the defense because it goes into a crowd of players rather than to a single, isolated *receiver*.

tight end — (A muscular back side.) His primary goals are catching passes and *blocking* for teammates on offense. He's typically located at the far reaches of the *line of scrimmage*. See *offensive end* and *split end*.

time-out — Ninety seconds used by a team to plan future game activities. When the ball is dead, a team can call a time-out three times during each half.

total offense — (A mistake, such as forgetting your birthday.) Determined by taking the rushing and passing yards gained and adding them together to get total yards. One of many of a game's *statistics*.

touchback — If the ball goes to the point where it reaches the *end zone* and goes past the end line on a kicking play other than a *field-goal* attempt, the officials then move the ball to the twenty-yard line for the offense to take *possession* there. A player also has the option of downing the ball in the *end zone* after retrieving it. His team then assumes possession on its own 20-yard line.

touchdown — (When you're able to reach below your knees.) Six points awarded for getting the ball over the other team's *goal line* by a *pass* or *run*. Another way of scoring those six points comes if a team scoops up a ball from the ground that's resting in the other team's *end zone*. See *TD*.

trap block — If executed correctly, this can be a successful *play* for an offense. The offense gets a player from the opponent's defensive line to commit, coming through the *front line*. At this point, the *offensive tacklers* come into play, knocking this defender out of the *play* with a swift *block*, leaving a nice gap for the ballcarrier to *run* through where that defender once was. See *mousetrap*.

triple option — (When three men ask you out for the same evening.) After examining the defense, the *quarterback* will decide on a given *play* to *pass* the football, use a *pitchout* to a running back who will take the ball to the outer portion of the *field*, or give the ball to a back who will *run* down the center of the *field*.

triple wing — (When you get three chicken wings from that dinner combo at the drive-thru.) Features a *tight end* in an offensive *formation* lining up as usual, but with the *fullback* several yards beyond and behind the *tight end*. Meanwhile, the *halfback* is also in the *backfield*, but in a spot in the *backfield* back several yards.

try for point — A chance for a team to earn extra points by running the ball into the *end zone*, passing it there, or kicking it after a *touchdown*. By kicking the ball through the *uprights*, a team gets one point. For those successful in running or passing the ball into the *end zone*, they get two points.

turn-in — (Go to sleep.) Designed to have the offensive *pass* catcher trot forward and abruptly turn toward the *field's* center to snag a *pass*.

turn-out — (Show up for an event.) Designed to have the offensive *pass* catcher trot forward and abruptly turn toward the *field's sideline* to snag a *pass*.

turnover — (A type of dessert.) When a squad fumbles the ball or gives up an interception and turns it over to the other team.

turn the corner — In a situation where the ballcarrier would like to get farther *downfield* he, early on in the *play*, heads across the *field* rather than down it, trying to move to the outer edges of the *play*. Once there, he can make a mad dash toward the other team's *end zone*.

two-minute drill — Also known as *two-minute offense* or *hurry-up offense*. A form of clock management during the final moments of a game when the offense realizes it doesn't have much time remaining to pull off a win. To maximize the time remaining, it has the *quarterback* map out the strategy for the next few *downs* during the *huddle*, rather than eating up time and calling a *huddle* repeatedly. See *hurry-up offense*.

two-platoon system — When a team has some players who only play on offense and others who only play on defense.

two-way player — (A date who can't decide if he wants to see you or not.) Sometimes known as a *sixty-minute player*. In these days of super specialization, there is little use of two-way players, who would appear in the entire game, no matter whether the offense was on the *field* or the defense. See *sixty-minute player*.

U

umpire — As part of the crew of officials, he monitors the *field* from his spot among the defenders in the *backfield*, checking for violations including *holding* situations, illegal equipment, and men *downfield* illegally on a *pass* or *kickoff play*.

unbalanced line — Occurs when one side of the *line*—the *center* being the middle of that *line*—has more players on its side than on the other side.

undershift — After examining an offense's setup, a defense may react by moving linemen to the other side of the defensive line, where there are fewer players, to stop a *play* they feel may go in that direction.

United States Football League — No longer a competitor to the *National Football League (NFL)* because it is now defunct. Once had teams that played during football's off-season.

unload — Also known as throw away, this is when the *quarterback* tosses a ball *downfield* after he sees defenders coming closer to him, and he fears losing *yardage* if he were to hold onto the ball for a *sack* rather than tossing the football elsewhere.

unnecessary roughness — (A polite way to say your kids are beating up on each other.) Results in a 15-yard *penalty* for things such as tripping, trying to *tackle* an opponent after he's left the playing *field*, or attacking an opponent who has no bearing on the *play* before or after the *play* is over.

unsportsmanlike conduct — (When your children punch each other in front of the neighbors.) A 15-yard *penalty* goes against the team for these violations, and a player committing these infractions may face ejection from the game. Violations include swearing on the *field*, hitting an official in any way, scuffling with another player on the *field*, or tackling a player not participating in the *play*.

upfield — Also known as *downfield*. Indicates the direction toward which the offense tries to go.

uprights — (At least two honorable people.) These attach to the *goalpost* and go up in the air vertically. They serve as a reference point for the kicker; he's trying to get the ball through them on a *field-goal* or *extra-point* try.

up top — When a team goes with a *play* designed to be a *pass*.

USFL — (An acronym for United States and Florida.) Acronym for the *United States Football League.*

W

waiver — (Someone who enjoys greeting others with movement of the hand.)- When a team releases a player, they often put him on waivers. As standard operating procedure, other *NFL* teams can pick that released player before the initial team that released him trades him or sends him elsewhere. To get the waived player, a team purchases his contract for the asking cost.

weak safety — (No long-term job security.) A roving player on defense whose job it is to assist his team on *run* or *pass plays* to any area of the *field*. At the start of a *play*, he usually positions himself across from the side with fewer players on the *offensive line*. See *free safety*.

weak side — Identifies a situation where there are fewer players on one side of the *line* than the other side. See *short side*.

wedge — Used by the player who's running back a *kickoff*. Players form a moving roadblock to give the returner as much chance as possible to make it *downfield*. This "roadblock" mows down players in the runner's way.

wide receiver — A player with a key responsibility of catching the football. He's at the far section of the offensive *line*, at the very end. See *split end, flanker*, or *spread end*.

wingback — (When they give you too many wings in your chicken assortment, and you'd prefer a back or two, instead.) Performing many roles, this player catches passes, runs with the ball, and blocks for teammates who have the ball. He lines up in back of the *end*, diagonally behind him, on the side of the *formation* with the most players.

wing T formation — An offensive *alignment* with the *halfback* situating himself on the right or left side of the *formation* to play *wingback*.

wishbone or wishbone T — (Type of salad dressing.) This places in the offensive *backfield* a *fullback* and two *halfbacks*, who play in back of the *fullback*, one on his right and the other on his left. This formation puts to work a *split end* and a *tight end*.

X

Xs and Os — Used by the coaching staff to show players, in a visual way, plays on offense that a team will use and how to defend against the opposition when they *run plays*. The Xs may represent the offense or defense of one team, the Os the opposite team.

Y

Yale coverage — (Ivy league news.) When a defense expects a *pass*, it will sometimes use the Yale coverage, which has two *safeties*, each responsible for guarding their side of the *field* by using a *zone* defense. Closer to the *line of scrimmage*, the defenders will play in a *man-to-man* defense.

yardage — (How much land you own.) A *statistic* to record the efforts of different players who carry, catch, or *pass* the ball. This *statistic* notes how far they went, for instance, in one particular game.

yardage chain — Also known as *sticks* or as a *chain*, this *chain*, moved by game personnel, is 10 yards long, the distance an offense must move in four plays to keep the ball. Game personnel keep the chain on the *sidelines* to see if, indeed, a team has gone that distance. See *sticks* and *chain*.

yard line — These are white lines at five-yard intervals stretching horizontally across the *field* with the purpose of letting the teams know how far it is to the *goal line*.

Z

zebra — (An animal at the zoo.) Affectionate term for the officials, who all wear a shirt with black-and-white stripes as a part of their uniform.

zone — As opposed to *man-to-man* coverage on defense, zone coverage emphasizes the defense taking a part of the *field*—rather than a particular player—and covering it.

zone blocking — Also known as *area blocking*, this strategy has the offense determine that each of its players is responsible for monitoring a part of the *field*. When a defender arrives there, the offensive player must *block* that opponent. See *area blocking*.

Printed in the United States
134719LV00017BA/210/A